THE FLOOD PREVENTION HANDBOOK

HOW TO PROTECT YOUR HOME & FAMILY WHEN WATERS RISE

THE FLOOD PREVENTION HANDBOOK

RYAN LEE PRICE

Published in 2026 by:
ULYSSES PRESS
an imprint of The Stable Book Group
32 Court Street, Suite 2109
Brooklyn, NY 11201
www.ulyssespress.com

Library of Congress Control Number: 2025944348
ISBN: 978-1-64604-847-2
eISBN: 978-1-64604-848-9

Managing editor: Claire Chun
Project editor: Renee Rutledge
Proofreader: Sherian Brown
Front cover design: what!design @ whatweb.com
Artwork: cover sandbags and water © thanatphotoo/shutterstock.com, chapter start caution tape © creativestockpro/shutterstock.com

Printed in the United States
10 9 8 7 6 5 4 3 2 1

CONTENTS

INTRODUCTION

Water is an essential resource; yet, when it exceeds its boundaries, it has the potential to cause devastation. Floods, hurricanes, and other water-related disasters are some of the most destructive forces of nature, and their frequency and severity have been rising in recent decades. As climate change accelerates, these disasters are becoming more common and their impacts more severe.

Flooding is the most persistent and costly natural disaster in the United States, with more than 24.4 million people in the US living in flood-prone areas, according to *Scientific Data*. Flooding results in billions of dollars in damage every year, and the National Flood Insurance Program (NFIP) has paid out over $87 billion in flood claims since its inception in 1968. The growing frequency of flooding events is largely attributed to the effects of climate change.

The link between climate change and increased flooding risk is well-documented. Abnormal rises in sea level can lead to devastating coastal flooding. As the climate warms, the atmosphere holds more moisture, leading to more torrential rainfalls and events like atmospheric rivers becoming more common. Additionally, melting glaciers and ice sheets are contributing to rising sea levels, exacerbating coastal flooding risks. The combination of these factors means that flood-prone regions will continue to face increased threats, and those threats will intensify.

Hurricanes, like Hurricane Katrina (2005), Hurricane Sandy (2012), and Hurricane Maria (2017), demonstrate the devastating impact of water-related disasters on communities. The economic toll of these storms is staggering. For example, the National Weather Service states Hurricane Katrina alone caused an estimated $125 billion in damages, making it one of the costliest natural disasters in US history.

While flooding from hurricanes is one of the most visible water-related disasters, flash floods and tsunamis also pose significant risks. Flash floods are notably dangerous because they can occur with very little warning. The Federal Emergency Management Agency (FEMA) warns that "just six inches of moving water can knock you down, and one foot of moving water can sweep your vehicle away." Tsunamis, though less frequent, can cause catastrophic damage in coastal areas, as seen in the 2004 Indian Ocean tsunami that claimed over 230,000 lives.

The increased frequency and intensity of water-related disasters are no longer a matter of speculation; they are the present reality.

IMPORTANCE OF PREPARATION

Preparation is critical to minimizing the risks associated with flooding, hurricanes, and other water-related disasters. The importance of preparing in advance cannot be overstated. According to FEMA's *Mitigation Ideas*, "mitigation—taking steps to reduce the impact of future disasters—can significantly reduce the loss of life and property damage." Being prepared can help protect not only your financial investment but also your emotional well-being and safety.

FINANCIAL BENEFITS

The financial costs of water-related disasters can be devastating. In addition to damage to homes and personal property, survivors must often contend with the high costs of evacuation, medical bills, and recovery. According to Climate.gov, in 2017, the United States experienced over $300 billion in damages from weather and climate disasters, with flooding alone accounting for over $80 billion of that total. One of the most important steps in mitigating the financial impact is purchasing flood insurance. However, flood damage is not typically covered by standard policies, so homeowners, particularly those living in flood-prone areas, should invest in a dedicated flood insurance policy. Without flood insurance, recovery can be slow and financially crippling.

Preparation protects personal property while also contributing to long-term economic stability. The National Institute of Building Sciences found that every federal dollar spent on disaster mitigation saves about six dollars in future disaster costs. This emphasizes that preparedness is a wise investment that ultimately saves homeowners, businesses, and governments significant amounts of money in the aftermath of disasters.

For renters, the financial strain from a flood can be just as devastating. Renters' insurance is essential for covering the loss of personal belongings during a flood. Renters often overlook this coverage, but it's a key part of ensuring that their personal property is safeguarded.

EMOTIONAL AND PSYCHOLOGICAL BENEFITS

Beyond the financial advantages, preparing for a flood or hurricane also has substantial emotional benefits. The anxiety and stress of not knowing how to protect your family or belongings during a disaster can be overwhelming. However, taking proactive steps to prepare can alleviate some of that anxiety.

When you know that your home is fortified and that you have an emergency kit, evacuation plan, and flood insurance in place, you're better equipped to handle the emotional strain of a disaster. Preparation provides a sense of control in an otherwise uncontrollable situation, helping to reduce feelings of panic and helplessness.

SAFETY BENEFITS

The most critical reason for preparation is safety. Proper planning can mean the difference between life and death. Ready.gov stresses that "evacuating early and knowing what to do before and during a disaster can save your life." The dangers of flooding and hurricanes are not just related to property damage—they also pose significant risks to human life. In flood scenarios, quick action can save lives, and knowing where to go and what to do can keep you and your loved ones from harm.

WHO THIS BOOK IS FOR

This book is for anyone concerned with protecting themself, their families, and their property from the rising risks associated with water-related disasters. Whether you're a homeowner, renter, or prospective buyer, the information here will help you understand the threats you face, take action to reduce risks, and recover from any water-related disaster that may occur.

Homeowners will benefit from practical advice and actionable steps to assess their property's flood risk, prepare their homes to withstand water damage, and ensure they have adequate insurance coverage. For homeowners in flood-prone areas, this book offers detailed guidance on mitigating flood risk through structural modifications, insurance, and emergency preparedness.

Renters will find valuable insights on protecting personal belongings, securing renters' insurance, and creating a flood-response plan. Even if you don't own the property you live in, there are steps you can take to safeguard your possessions and ensure your family's safety during a flood.

Prospective homebuyers will gain the knowledge needed to evaluate the flood risks of a potential new home. From understanding flood zones to recognizing signs of water damage, this book will help you make an informed decision before purchasing a property.

In the pages that follow, you will learn how to assess flood risks, implement effective preparation strategies, and recover after a disaster. By taking action today, you can ensure a safer future for yourself, your loved ones, and your community. The time to prepare is now.

CHAPTER 1

PURCHASING OR RENTING A FLOOD-SAFE HOME

Purchasing or renting a home is one of the most significant decisions you will make, and understanding the potential risks associated with flooding is essential, particularly in today's environment, where natural disasters, including floods, are becoming more frequent and severe.

The effects of flood damage extend far beyond the immediate destruction of property. Homeowners and renters may face not only devastating financial losses but also prolonged displacements, emotional stress, and the possibility of long-term health and safety hazards. In flood-prone regions, these risks are even more pronounced, as flooding events can lead to significant disruption in daily life and require costly repairs that are not always covered by standard homeowner's insurance policies. In light of these challenges, assessing a property's flood risk before making a purchase or signing a lease is critical. Armed with this knowledge, prospective buyers and renters can confidently assess whether a home is flood-safe and whether the surrounding neighborhood is adequately prepared for potential flooding.

HOW TO IDENTIFY POTENTIAL FLOOD ZONES

Identifying whether a property lies within a flood-prone area is the first crucial step in evaluating its flood risk. This process can seem overwhelming, especially for first-time homebuyers or renters unfamiliar with flood-related issues. However, a variety of accessible resources and methods can provide a clear picture.

FEDERAL AND LOCAL RESOURCES

The FEMA Flood Map Service Center provides flood maps that categorize properties based on their likelihood of experiencing a flood. These maps divide flood zones into categories, each indicating the level of risk.

Floodplain maps show the extent of areas likely to flood based on various conditions, including topography, rainfall patterns, and historical flood data. FEMA's flood maps are some of the most commonly used tools for determining flood risk in a given area.

- **Zone AE or A1–A30:** These high-risk flood zones are areas that have a 1 percent annual chance of flooding. If a property falls into one of these zones, flood insurance is typically required by lenders for federally backed loans. Properties in these zones are particularly susceptible to riverine flooding and other types of severe water damage.
- **Zone X (shaded):** Areas in this zone face a moderate risk of flooding, with a 0.2 percent annual chance of flooding. Homes in this zone may not be required to carry flood insurance, but it is still advisable to assess the potential for flooding in the event of a heavy storm or other extreme weather event.
- **Zone X (unshaded):** These areas are typically considered low-to-moderate risk and have minimal flooding likelihood. While flood insurance may not be required in these areas, it is still a wise choice for homeowners to consider coverage, particularly in light of increasing flood risks due to climate change.

- **Zone VE:** Areas, located along coasts, are considered at risk for both storm surge and flooding.

To access FEMA's maps:

1. Visit the FEMA Flood Map Service Center website at msc.fema.gov.
2. Enter the property's address to view the flood-zone classification and details about the area's flood risk.
3. Review the map's information, including the base flood elevation (BFE), which indicates the minimum elevation to which buildings in the area must be elevated to minimize flood risks.

It is important to note that FEMA's flood zones are subject to change over time. As climate change and urban development continue to alter natural water flow, flood zones may be revised, and new areas may be designated as flood prone. As such, staying up to date with FEMA's maps is essential for anyone evaluating flood risks.

Beyond FEMA's resources, local government offices and municipal planning departments often maintain valuable flood-risk information. These agencies typically collect and analyze data about local flooding patterns, stormwater management systems, and flood-mitigation strategies. They may also offer access to historical flood records and provide insights into how previous floods have affected specific areas.

In some regions, floodplain ordinances and building codes can provide additional guidance on the level of flood preparedness within a community. For example, cities located in coastal or river-adjacent areas may have regulations that restrict development in floodplains, require elevated building foundations, or mandate the use of flood-resistant materials in construction. By contacting local building departments or visiting their websites, prospective buyers and renters can gather information about how well a neighborhood has been prepared for flooding.

Additionally, local libraries and historical societies can be useful resources for gathering historical flood data. These institutions often maintain archives with records of past flood events, including photographs, newspaper clippings, and reports. Inquiring with these organizations can provide a sense of how often the area has experienced flooding, the extent of the damage, and whether flooding has worsened over time due to urban development or environmental factors.

RESEARCHING A PROPERTY'S FLOOD HISTORY

Understanding a property's specific flood history is just as important as evaluating the flood risks in the broader community. If a property has experienced previous flooding, it may be more vulnerable to future water damage. This can affect the property's structural integrity and, potentially, its market value. However, gathering information on a property's flood history can be challenging, as disclosure laws vary by location, and sellers or landlords may not always provide full details.

The NFIP, administered by FEMA, requires property owners who purchase flood insurance to disclose claims history. This means that if a home has experienced flooding in the past and the owner filed a claim, it should be documented and available. However, this requirement does not always extend to renters or property buyers, and in many states, sellers are not legally obligated to voluntarily disclose past flood damage unless specifically asked. Therefore, it is essential to be proactive when seeking information about a property's flood history.

Start by asking direct questions of the seller, landlord, or real estate agent. Inquire about any previous flooding incidents, water damage, or insurance claims related to flooding. It's also useful to ask whether the property has been elevated above the BFE. Even if the property has not flooded in the past, these questions can provide insight into the level of preparedness and whether the property has been retrofitted to withstand potential floods.

In many states, disclosure statements are legally required. These statements typically outline known risks and past incidents of flooding, along with other potential hazards like radon, lead, or asbestos levels. Look for language such as "recurrent flooding," "water intrusion," or "moisture-related damage." If any of these terms appear, it's an indication that the property may be vulnerable to flooding in the future.

Hiring a professional inspector can provide an objective and thorough evaluation. Home inspectors with experience in flood damage can identify subtle signs of water intrusion, such as water stains, warped flooring, or musty odors. Additionally, some inspectors specialize in flood risk and can evaluate whether the property's infrastructure, such as its drainage systems and foundation, is designed to withstand future flooding events.

USING ONLINE TOOLS

In recent years, various online resources have become available to help prospective homeowners and renters assess flood risks more conveniently. Websites such as FloodFactor.com aggregate flood-risk data from FEMA, NOAA, and other sources. By entering an address, users can access comprehensive reports on the property's flood history and the likelihood of future flooding.

For example, FloodFactor.com provides an interactive map that includes information on a property's past flood events, flood insurance claims, and local flood-mitigation efforts. This platform also estimates the future risk of flooding based on climate projections, such as rising sea levels and more frequent severe weather events.

In addition to private resources, NOAA offers detailed flood-risk assessments, including forecasts, historical data, and climate change projections. These assessments can help you understand how long-term environmental changes may affect flood risk in specific regions.

While no home can be entirely flood-proof, identifying flood-prone areas and taking steps to mitigate risk can provide invaluable peace of mind for homeowners and renters alike.

KEY INDICATORS OF FLOOD RISK IN A NEIGHBORHOOD

When considering purchasing or renting a home, it's crucial to look beyond the property itself. The surrounding neighborhood can also significantly impact the property's vulnerability to flooding. Various environmental and infrastructural factors contribute to the flood risk in any given area, and recognizing these early can save you from unexpected and costly challenges. Understanding key indicators, from proximity to bodies of water to design and availability of local drainage systems, can provide critical insights into how likely it is that a neighborhood will experience flooding. This knowledge allows you to make more informed decisions about where to live, what kind of insurance to purchase, and how to prepare for potential water-related disasters.

PROXIMITY TO BODIES OF WATER

The first and most obvious factor that influences flood risk is the proximity to bodies of water, such as rivers, lakes, oceans, or reservoirs. While living near water can offer beautiful views and recreational opportunities, it inherently increases the risk of flooding, especially in times of heavy rainfall or storm surges.

RIVERS AND STREAMS: Riverine flooding, or flooding that occurs when rivers overflow due to excessive rainfall or snowmelt, is one of the most common types of flood events. Locations near a river or stream come with an increased risk of flooding, particularly after prolonged rain or a rapid snowmelt. Proximity to river tributaries can also make a property more vulnerable to flash floods, which can occur suddenly due to localized rainfall.

COASTAL AREAS: Coastlines face increased vulnerability to storm surges and tidal flooding, both of which are amplified by rising sea levels. Coastal flooding can result from hurricanes, tropical storms, or even high tides. As climate change accelerates, rising sea levels are causing coastal areas to flood more frequently. FEMA's Coastal Barrier Resources System (CBRS) maps provide additional information on areas at risk of storm surges.

RESERVOIRS AND DAMS: If a property is located downstream from a reservoir or dam, it faces the heightened risk of dam failure or overflow, which can lead to catastrophic flooding. Even though dams are generally built with flood control in mind, they can still fail due to structural weaknesses or extreme weather events. Local emergency management offices typically have safety records and procedures for flood risk related to reservoirs and dams, and it is advisable to inquire about the safety and maintenance of these structures before purchasing or renting a home in such an area.

DRAINAGE AND STORMWATER SYSTEMS

Beyond natural bodies of water, the drainage and stormwater management systems in a neighborhood play a crucial role in its ability to handle heavy rainfall and prevent flooding. Poorly designed or maintained drainage systems can result in water accumulating in streets and homes, even in areas that aren't typically considered high-risk for flooding.

CLOGGED DRAINS: Urban and suburban neighborhoods often rely on storm drains to carry away rainwater and prevent flooding. However, when these drains become clogged with debris, leaves, or waste, they lose their ability to channel water efficiently. As a result, the risk of localized flooding increases, especially during periods of heavy rain. Homebuyers and renters should inspect the condition of nearby storm drains or culverts and inquire with local authorities about the maintenance schedules for these drainage systems.

SLOPE AND TERRAIN: The natural slope of the land also influences how water flows through a neighborhood. Areas situated at the bottom of a valley or along low-lying terrain are more likely to collect runoff from nearby hills or mountains. Conversely, homes on elevated ground or on ridges tend to experience less flooding, as they are less likely to be directly impacted by rising water levels. When evaluating a property's flood risk, it's important to consider its relative elevation within the neighborhood and the surrounding terrain.

IMPERVIOUS SURFACES

Impervious surfaces, such as asphalt, concrete, and other nonporous materials, prevent rainwater from soaking into the ground. In neighborhoods with significant development, particularly in urban areas, the high concentration of impervious surfaces leads to greater runoff and a higher likelihood of flooding. This is particularly true for neighborhoods with little green space or natural features that allow water to infiltrate the soil.

Areas with high-density development and extensive road networks often experience flash flooding because there is less room for rainwater to be absorbed by the ground. If a neighborhood has undergone significant urbanization without adequate stormwater management, flooding risks are likely higher.

On the other hand, neighborhoods that incorporate green spaces, wetlands, trees, and grassy areas can act as natural barriers against flooding. These features absorb water and help manage runoff, which can mitigate the risk of flooding in the area. Properties surrounded by natural buffers tend to have lower flood risk because they benefit from the environmental function of these features.

LOCAL FLOOD DEFENSES

Many neighborhoods, particularly those in flood-prone regions, are equipped with flood defenses such as levees, sea walls, or stormwater-detention basins, and natural features like wetlands. These systems, often managed by local governments or flood-management agencies, form the first line of protection against flooding in neighborhoods and are designed to prevent or reduce flood damage by controlling the flow of water during heavy rainfall or storm surges. While flood defenses can significantly reduce the risk of flooding, they are not foolproof. If not properly maintained, or if they are overwhelmed by extreme weather events, these systems may fail, leading to widespread damage. Understanding their presence, effectiveness, and maintenance is essential for evaluating a neighborhood's overall flood resilience.

Local regulations also play a key role in managing stormwater runoff, a major contributor to urban flooding. Effective stormwater management codes typically include limits on impervious surfaces, such as concrete driveways, to reduce runoff and improve drainage. This helps to ensure better water absorption and less strain on drainage systems.

Additionally, regulations may require retention systems, like rainwater harvesting systems or detention basins, for new developments to manage runoff on site. These systems capture excess stormwater and release it gradually, reducing the risk of localized flooding. Landscaping standards also encourage the use of native plants and green infrastructure to further enhance water absorption. Neighborhoods that implement these measures are better equipped to manage heavy rainfall and prevent their drainage systems from being overwhelmed.

Understanding a neighborhood's flood history provides valuable insights into its vulnerability and the effectiveness of its flood-mitigation efforts.

LEVEES, SEA WALLS, AND FLOODWALLS

Levees, sea walls, and floodwalls are engineered structures designed to contain or divert floodwaters. While they can significantly reduce flood risks, their effectiveness depends on design, maintenance, and capacity.

Levees are earthen embankments constructed along rivers or coastlines to prevent water from overflowing into residential areas. According to the US Army Corps of Engineers, levees protect about 14 million people in the United States. However, regular maintenance is essential to ensure their continued effectiveness.

Made of concrete or steel, floodwalls serve a similar purpose but are typically used in urban areas where space is limited. Their ability to withstand floodwaters depends on proper design and maintenance.

When assessing a neighborhood, inquire about the existence of levees or floodwalls and check with local authorities for information on their maintenance schedules, capacity, and performance during past floods.

STORMWATER DRAINAGE SYSTEMS

An efficient stormwater drainage system is crucial for managing runoff and preventing flooding, particularly in urban areas where impermeable surfaces like roads and buildings prevent water absorption. These systems, including storm drains, sewers, and basins, channel and manage stormwater to reduce flooding risks. It's essential to assess the condition of these systems when evaluating flood preparedness in a neighborhood.

Storm drains and sewers direct rainwater away from streets and properties to larger bodies of water or to drainage basins. Regular cleaning is necessary to prevent blockages from debris, which can increase flood risks. Retention and detention basins further alleviate flooding by temporarily storing excess water and slowly releasing it, reducing peak flood levels.

Green infrastructure, such as permeable pavements, rain gardens, and bioswales, offers a sustainable solution by promoting water absorption and reducing runoff. These features allow water to infiltrate the ground, lessening the burden on storm drains and improving water quality by filtering pollutants.

When assessing a neighborhood's stormwater management, observe the presence of these systems and inquire about maintenance practices. Well-maintained systems are increasingly important as climate change intensifies storm patterns. An efficient stormwater drainage system, combining traditional infrastructure with green solutions, is key to minimizing flood risks and enhancing a community's resilience to flooding.

NATURAL FLOOD DEFENSES

Natural features like wetlands, mangroves, and forests play a significant role in flood mitigation. For instance, wetlands absorb excess water like a sponge, which can reduce flood peaks. Research by NOAA found that coastal wetlands in the US prevented over $625 million in flood damage during Hurricane Sandy in 2012.

Assess whether the neighborhood benefits from such natural defenses and whether there are conservation efforts in place to maintain them. The loss of these features due to urbanization or climate change can increase flood risks.

INTERPRETING ZONING ORDINANCES

Local zoning laws help to regulate how land is used and developed, especially in flood-prone areas. These ordinances ensure that construction in flood zones is done in a way that reduces risk and minimizes damage.

BUILDING CODES: In high-risk flood zones, building codes may require specific construction techniques, such as elevated foundations, flood vents, or flood-resistant materials. These regulations are designed to ensure that new buildings are less vulnerable to flood damage.

SETBACK REQUIREMENTS: Many flood zones require that homes be set back a certain distance from rivers, lakes, or coastlines to prevent flood damage. Setbacks help reduce the risk of erosion and provide additional space for floodwater to flow without impacting properties.

RESTRICTIONS ON DEVELOPMENT: In areas designated as wetlands or floodways (the main channels for floodwaters), local governments may restrict or even prohibit development to preserve natural floodplains and reduce the impact of flood events.

FOUNDATION AND HOUSE PLANS: BUILDING OR CHOOSING A FLOOD-SAFE HOME

When considering a home in a flood-prone area, the foundation and overall design are critical to minimizing flood damage. Whether building from scratch or evaluating an existing property, making the right choices in terms of the foundation, elevation, and design features that mitigate water damage can help reduce the likelihood of costly repairs, increase occupant safety, and protect your investment in the long term.

WHAT TO LOOK FOR IN A FLOOD-SAFE FOUNDATION

The foundation of a home serves as its structural base, and in flood-prone areas, it must be designed to withstand the destructive forces of water. A flood-safe foundation reduces water intrusion and enhances the home's overall stability.

RAISED FOUNDATIONS

Raising the foundation of a home above potential floodwaters is one of the most effective strategies for flood protection. There are several types of raised foundations commonly used in flood-resistant construction:

PIER AND BEAM FOUNDATIONS: In this design, the home is elevated above the ground on piers or columns embedded deep into the soil. This allows floodwaters to flow underneath the house without causing damage to the structure. This type of foundation is especially useful in coastal areas that experience storm surges or high tides.

PILES OR STILTS: Similar to pier and beam foundations, homes built on stilts are raised several feet above the ground. This design is often used in hurricane-prone regions where homes are exposed to both flooding and high winds. Stilts are usually constructed from durable materials like reinforced concrete, steel, or treated wood.

CRAWLSPACES: A crawlspace foundation elevates the house slightly above ground level, creating an area beneath the home that may be used for storage. These crawlspaces can be equipped with flood vents that allow water to flow through the space, reducing hydrostatic pressure and preventing damage during flooding.

FLOOD VENTS

Also known as foundation vents or flood openings, flood vents are crucial for homes in flood-prone areas, particularly those with enclosed foundations. These vents allow water to flow freely in and out of the foundation area, helping to prevent foundation failure caused by rising water pressure. Key features to look for in flood vents include automatic activation, where vents open when water levels rise, compliance with FEMA's sizing requirements (one square inch of venting per square foot of enclosed area), and materials resistant to corrosion, such as stainless steel or aluminum.

In addition to flood vents, waterproofing the foundation is an effective measure to prevent water intrusion. This can be achieved using waterproof membranes applied to the exterior of the foundation to block seepage, hydrophobic additives mixed into concrete to enhance its water resistance, and sealing all joints and cracks with waterproof caulk or epoxy to prevent water from entering. These combined strategies help ensure the foundation remains protected during flood events.

THE IMPORTANCE OF ELEVATION

Elevation is one of the most effective ways to reduce flood risk, as the higher a home is built above anticipated flood levels, the less likely it is to experience significant damage. The BFE is a key measurement used in floodplain management, indicating the height floodwaters are expected to reach during a 100-year flood event. Homes built above the BFE are less vulnerable to flooding. Freeboard, which involves elevating the home several feet above the BFE, adds an extra safety margin. Many local building codes now require at least one or two feet of freeboard in high-risk flood zones, which can also reduce flood insurance premiums by up to 25 percent.

In addition to raising the home itself, the land surrounding the property can be graded or sloped to direct water away from the foundation and prevent localized flooding. Grading involves shaping the ground so that water flows downward from the house, helping to prevent localized flooding and directing runoff away from the structure. Elevation doesn't only apply to the structure; it should also be factored into access points like doors, windows, and garages. Some important elevated features include:

- **Raised Front Steps or Ramps:** These entryways are above the flood level.
- **Raised Garages:** Elevated garages with sloped driveways prevent water from entering.
- **Elevated Window Wells:** These reduce the risk of water pooling around basement windows.

HOUSE DESIGN FEATURES THAT MITIGATE WATER DAMAGE

House design plays a critical role in reducing potential water damage and aiding in recovery after a flood. Key considerations include elevating vital systems, using water-resistant materials, reinforcing roofs, and incorporating flood-resilient features into the interior.

Elevating electrical systems is essential for reducing the risk of damage from floods. Electrical outlets, switches, and circuit breakers should be installed at least 12 inches above the base flood elevation to prevent submersion. Ground-fault circuit interrupter (GFCI) outlets are recommended to automatically cut power when water or electrical faults are detected, preventing electrocution or fire hazards. Similarly, HVAC systems should be elevated above flood levels, either by mounting them on raised platforms or placing them in attics.

Using water-resistant materials throughout the home is another critical flood-mitigation strategy. For flooring, materials like tile, concrete, and waterproof vinyl are ideal because they resist water damage better than carpet or wood. Wall systems should incorporate water-resistant drywall treated with fiberglass and waterproof insulation like closed-cell spray foam. Kitchen and bathroom cabinetry should be made from materials such as stainless steel or marine-grade plywood, which are highly resistant to water damage.

Reinforcing the roof is vital for protecting the home during heavy storms, which often bring flooding. A roof should be anchored with hurricane straps or clips to withstand high winds, and impact-resistant materials like metal or composite shingles can protect against flying debris. Proper drainage is also essential, as gutters and downspouts should direct rainwater away from the foundation to prevent localized flooding.

Backflow prevention systems are crucial to preventing sewer lines from backing up during floods. Installing backflow valves blocks reverse water flow and keeps contaminated water from entering the home's plumbing system. A sump pump with a battery backup is another effective tool to remove water that accumulates in basements or crawlspaces, especially during power outages.

Inside the home, elevating appliances such as refrigerators and washing machines on platforms keeps them above potential flood levels. Open floor plans are also beneficial, as they make it easier to clean up water and minimize the buildup of debris. Additionally, removable flooring systems that can be easily cleaned and replaced after a flood help reduce long-term damage.

Windows and doors should also be designed to handle both flooding and high winds. Hurricane-resistant glass can withstand flying debris and extreme winds, while flood-resistant doors, sealed with watertight gaskets, prevent water from entering the home.

These measures not only protect property and ensure the safety of residents but also reduce the long-term financial burden of flood damage. Prioritizing flood-safe design is an investment in long-term security, providing peace of mind in the face of rising flood risks due to climate change.

FLOODPLAIN MANAGEMENT ORDINANCES

Many communities participate in the NFIP, which regulates development in flood-prone areas. These ordinances typically include specific guidelines designed to reduce flood risks. For example, new or substantially improved buildings must be elevated above the base flood elevation, ensuring they are less likely to be affected by floodwaters. Additionally, flood-resistant foundation design standards, such as using pilings or columns, are often required in high-risk flood zones to ensure structural integrity during flood events.

Furthermore, these ordinances impose development restrictions to protect natural water flow, particularly by limiting construction in floodways, where building could obstruct the movement of floodwaters. To assess a neighborhood's compliance with these regulations, it's advisable to check with local zoning or planning departments. Communities that go beyond the NFIP's minimum standards may qualify for the FEMA's Community Rating System (CRS), which can provide residents with discounted flood insurance premiums, offering both financial and environmental benefits.

INSPECTION AND ENFORCEMENT

Strong building codes can only protect against flooding if they are properly enforced. When evaluating a neighborhood, find out if regular inspections are conducted on existing infrastructure and new developments to ensure compliance with flood-resistant standards. Additionally, penalty systems should be in place for violations of floodplain management or stormwater regulations, providing deterrents for noncompliance.

Public engagement is also crucial in promoting flood preparedness. Communities that involve residents in education programs and encourage participation in flood-risk mitigation efforts are more resilient to flooding. Local government websites, building departments, and community organizations are great resources for gathering information on enforcement practices and community involvement in flood prevention.

HOW TO INQUIRE ABOUT FLOOD HISTORY

Understanding a neighborhood's flood history provides critical insights into its vulnerability and the effectiveness of its flood defenses. This information can help you assess whether living there aligns with your risk tolerance and preparedness goals.

TALK TO POTENTIAL NEIGHBORS

Current residents can be an invaluable source of firsthand information about a neighborhood's flood history. When speaking with residents:

- **Ask Open-Ended Questions:** Initiate conversations by asking residents about their personal experiences with flooding. Encourage them to share details on the frequency and severity of past floods, as well as the impact these events have had on their properties and the community as a whole. Understanding local histories of flooding can provide valuable context for identifying areas at higher risk and gauging the effectiveness of current flood-mitigation efforts.
- **Explore Patterns:** In addition to asking about individual experiences, probe into whether specific locations, such as particular streets, prop-

erties, or neighborhoods, are known to flood regularly. Residents may have observed patterns that indicate higher vulnerability to flooding in certain spots, helping you understand if certain areas need targeted interventions or improved flood-protection measures.

- **Gauge Community Preparedness:** It's also important to understand how well-prepared the community is for flooding events. Ask residents about their personal flood preparedness practices, as well as whether there's a culture of collaboration during emergencies. Do neighbors help each other with sandbagging or evacuations? Are there local volunteer groups or emergency response networks? A community that is proactive and well-prepared can significantly reduce the risks and damages associated with floods.

Building relationships with neighbors not only helps you gather information but also connects you to a potential support network during crises.

CONSULT REAL ESTATE AGENTS

Real estate agents are often required by law to disclose known flood risks associated with a property. When working with an agent, ask about:

- **Disclosure Requirements:** Investigate the legal obligations for disclosing flood risks in the area. Many regions have specific laws requiring property sellers to inform buyers about past flooding events or flood-risk assessments. Understanding the disclosure requirements can help ensure that you're receiving accurate and complete information about the flood risk associated with a property.
- **Flood Insurance History:** Ask whether the property is currently covered by flood insurance. If flood insurance is in place, it could indicate that the property is located in a high-risk flood zone, or it may suggest a history of prior flood events. In some cases, flood insurance coverage may be mandated by the lender if the property is in a designated flood zone. Reviewing the property's flood insurance history can provide insights into its vulnerability and whether flood damage has been an ongoing concern.

- **Previous Repairs:** Inquire about any past repairs that were made due to flood damage. Were these repairs completed in compliance with current flood-resistant standards, such as elevating the structure above the BFE or using flood-resistant materials? Understanding whether the repairs were made according to proper regulations can give you an idea of the property's preparedness for future flooding and whether it has been adequately fortified against future risks.

While real estate agents can provide useful insights, it's essential to verify their information through independent research.

ACCESS LOCAL RECORDS

As mentioned, local government offices and agencies maintain records that can shed light on a neighborhood's flood history. Key resources include:

- **Floodplain Maps:** FEMA's Flood Map Service Center offers detailed flood maps that show flood zones, risk levels, and base flood elevations. (See page 65.)
- **Historic Flood Reports:** Many municipalities maintain records through planning or public works departments that document past flooding events. These reports often provide insights into the frequency, severity, and areas most affected by floods. Reviewing this historical data can help gauge the long-term flood risks for a specific neighborhood or property and may highlight patterns that influence future flood mitigation strategies.
- **Drainage System Assessments:** Engineering studies or maintenance records for local drainage systems can reveal potential vulnerabilities within the community's infrastructure. These assessments may highlight weaknesses such as inadequate stormwater management systems, outdated drainage infrastructure, or areas that are prone to flooding during heavy rain events. Understanding the capacity and condition of local drainage systems can give you a clearer picture of how well-prepared the area is to handle floodwaters.

Additionally, many local governments now offer online portals where residents can access this information. Check your local government's websites to see if they offer such services.

GATHER PROFESSIONAL ASSESSMENTS

For a comprehensive evaluation, consider hiring a flood risk assessor or engineer. These professionals can provide:

- **Site-Specific Analysis:** This involves a detailed evaluation of the property's unique characteristics, including its elevation, proximity to flood-prone areas, and potential drainage issues. Such an analysis can provide recommendations on how to minimize flood damage, such as elevating the structure, reinforcing the foundation, or improving landscaping to direct water away from the property.
- **Historical Data Review:** This review can include past flood insurance claims, repair records, and community-wide flood history.
- **Insurance Impact Assessment:** Insurance providers typically assess flood risk based on the property's past exposure to floods, the effectiveness of existing flood protection measures, and the area's flood zone classification. This assessment can help homeowners understand potential increases in flood insurance costs and explore mitigation steps to reduce those premiums.

A neighborhood's preparedness for flooding plays a critical role in the safety, resilience, and quality of life for its residents. By evaluating community flood defenses, understanding local building codes, and researching flood history, prospective buyers and renters can make informed decisions about where to live. A well-prepared neighborhood is more than just a collection of homes; it is a community dedicated to minimizing risk, protecting residents, and recovering quickly from natural disasters.

CHAPTER 2

UNDERSTANDING FLOOD INSURANCE

In the United States, floods are among the most common and costly natural disasters, affecting hundreds of thousands of homes and causing billions of dollars in property damage each year. As climate change accelerates, bringing more intense storms and rising sea levels, flood risk is projected to increase significantly across both coastal and inland areas. In this context, understanding the nuances of flood insurance becomes essential for anyone purchasing or renting a home, particularly in or near flood-prone zones. This chapter explains why standard homeowner's insurance does not cover flood damage, explores the vital role of separate flood insurance policies, and helps readers make informed decisions about protecting their homes and assets.

WHY STANDARD HOMEOWNER'S INSURANCE DOESN'T COVER FLOOD DAMAGE

One of the most widespread misconceptions about homeowner's insurance is that it automatically covers all types of water-related damage. While typical homeowners policies may include coverage for certain types of water incidents, such as burst pipes or a malfunctioning water heater, they almost universally exclude flood damage. This exclusion stems from the nature of flood risks and the systemic challenge they present to insurance models.

Flooding is considered a catastrophic risk event. It often affects large geographical areas and can damage or destroy thousands of homes at once. Insurance companies, operating under traditional risk models that rely on a diversified pool of claimants, cannot feasibly spread the risk of a massive flood event across their customer base without incurring severe losses. As a result, most private insurers exclude flood damage from standard homeowners policies to protect their solvency and manage risk exposure.

This exclusion was starkly evident in the aftermath of major flood events like Hurricane Harvey in 2017. The storm dumped more than 50 inches of rain in parts of southeastern Texas, flooding over 200,000 homes in the Houston area alone. An alarming number of affected homeowners did not have flood insurance, mistakenly believing their standard policies would offer coverage. Consequently, many families were left with overwhelming repair costs and limited federal aid.

Even in less severe flood events, the financial burden of recovery can be substantial. According to FEMA, just one inch of floodwater can cause as much as $25,000 in home damages. For properties located outside designated high-risk zones, where flood insurance is not federally mandated, homeowners often underestimate their vulnerability and forgo purchasing additional protection. This is a decision that can prove financially devastating.

THE IMPORTANCE OF HAVING A SEPARATE FLOOD INSURANCE POLICY

Given the gap in coverage from standard policies, obtaining a separate flood insurance policy is the only effective way to safeguard one's property from flood-related losses. Flood insurance is available through both the NFIP and, increasingly, through private insurance providers who are developing alternative products.

The NFIP was created in 1968 to offer homeowners, renters, businesses and more affordable flood insurance, while also encouraging people to follow floodplain management regulations. NFIP policies cover both building and contents, with separate coverage limits. As of 2023, the maximum coverage for residential buildings is $250,000, while contents coverage is capped at $100,000. These policies typically have a 30-day waiting period before becoming active, which means that homeowners must plan ahead and cannot rely on last-minute enrollment before an impending storm.

Flood insurance under the NFIP can be purchased through a network of participating insurance companies and agents. Premium rates are determined based on a variety of factors, from the property's flood zone designation to the history of flood claims on the property.

THE PROPERTY'S FLOOD ZONE DESIGNATION

Flood zones are geographic areas defined by FEMA that reflect varying levels of flood risk. These zones appear on Flood Insurance Rate Maps (FIRMs) and are used by the NFIP to assess insurance requirements and calculate premiums.

Flood zones fall into general categories:

- **High-Risk Zones:** Labeled as Zone A or Zone V (coastal areas), these are areas with a 1 percent chance of flooding annually (also known as the 100-year floodplain). See Risk Levels and Probabilities on page 62. Homeowners with federally backed mortgages in these zones are required to carry flood insurance.
- **Moderate- to Low-Risk Zones:** Labeled as Zone B, C, or X, these areas have a lower probability of flooding, but not zero. Approximately 20 percent of flood insurance claims originate in these so-called "low-risk" zones.
- **Undetermined Risk Areas:** Areas without detailed flood hazard analyses, often labeled as Zone D, reflect unknown risk levels.

Premiums are significantly higher in high-risk zones than in moderate- or low-risk zones. Furthermore, under FEMA's new Risk Rating 2.0 pricing methodology (see page 28), effective nationwide as of 2022, rates are now based on more granular, property-specific factors rather than simply which flood zone a property is located in. However, zone designation still influences regulatory requirements, such as whether flood insurance is mandatory.

After Hurricane Harvey, over 70 percent of the properties flooded in the Houston area were located outside the designated high-risk flood zones; this demonstrates that flood maps do not always predict where water will go. Many homeowners who skipped insurance due to being in a "low-risk" zone suffered devastating financial losses.

ELEVATION RELATIVE TO BASE FLOOD ELEVATION

A structure's BFE is a critical factor in determining its flood risk and, consequently, the cost of insurance premiums. For example, if the BFE for a property is 10 feet, and the home's lowest floor is at eight feet, the structure is considered two feet below the base flood elevation. This increases both the risk of flooding and the cost of insurance.

- Structures built at or above the BFE are generally considered less risky and therefore qualify for lower premiums.
- Structures below the BFE are at higher risk and will face much higher premium rates under NFIP guidelines.

Homeowners may submit an elevation certificate, prepared by a licensed surveyor or engineer, to their insurer to verify the structure's elevation. This certificate includes crucial information such as the lowest floor elevation, the building type, and the location of key structural systems. Even under Risk Rating 2.0, elevation remains a relevant factor, especially for properties in high-risk areas.

Homeowners with buildings elevated above the BFE often qualify for substantial premium discounts. In some cases, elevating a home by even a foot or two can reduce flood insurance costs by thousands of dollars annually. In the aftermath of disasters, FEMA often encourages or funds elevation projects as part of mitigation grants to reduce future claims.

In the New Jersey Shore area post-Hurricane Sandy, FEMA recommended elevating homes to meet or exceed new BFEs. Homeowners who took advantage of mitigation programs not only reduced future risk but also substantially lowered their NFIP premiums.

BUILDING STRUCTURE, AGE, AND MATERIALS

The physical characteristics of the building being insured also weigh heavily in determining the premium. The NFIP assesses several building-specific factors:

- **Construction Materials:** Wood-frame structures tend to sustain more flood damage than buildings made of masonry or concrete, influencing premium costs.
- **Foundation Type:** Homes with **basements** or **crawlspaces** are considered higher-risk due to increased likelihood of water intrusion, whereas elevated structures on piers or posts may qualify for lower rates.
- **Age of the Building:** Structures built before the community adopted a FEMA Flood Insurance Rate Map (known as pre-FIRM structures) may be subject to different rating criteria. Post-FIRM buildings, constructed in compliance with modern floodplain regulations, often benefit from better rates due to reduced vulnerability. Older buildings, on the other hand, may not be in compliance with modern codes and can be assessed significantly higher premiums unless retrofitting is undertaken.
- **Number of Floors and Occupancy Type:** A single-family home will be rated differently from a duplex or apartment complex. Multistory homes may have different rates based on how much of the structure is below the BFE.

A two-story brick home built in 2018 on elevated piers in Miami, Florida, will be significantly cheaper to insure through the NFIP than a single-story wood-frame bungalow built in 1970 without elevation measures in a similar location.

HISTORY OF FLOOD CLAIMS ON THE PROPERTY

In October 2021, FEMA introduced a new pricing methodology called Risk Rating 2.0, which aims to make flood insurance more actuarially sound and equitable. Unlike the previous system, which relied heavily on flood zones and elevation certificates, Risk Rating 2.0 uses advanced modeling techniques and property-specific characteristics to determine rates. The result is a more precise reflection of a property's unique risk profile. While Risk Rating 2.0 has led to premium increases for some policyholders, it has also lowered costs for others who were previously overpaying relative to their actual risk.

Private flood insurance options have also expanded in recent years. These alternatives may offer higher coverage limits, customizable policies, and shorter waiting periods. However, private flood insurance is not available in all areas, and not all mortgage lenders accept it as a substitute for NFIP coverage in mandatory flood zones. Homebuyers and renters should consult with their lenders, real estate professionals, and insurance agents to explore available options and ensure compliance with all requirements.

Flood insurance is especially critical for those living in high-risk areas, but even homes located outside of designated flood zones should not be complacent. Remember, FEMA estimates that more than 20 percent of NFIP claims come from properties located in moderate- to low-risk areas. Flash flooding, infrastructure failure, and changing weather patterns can all contribute to unexpected inundation in regions previously thought to be safe.

In addition to covering structural damage and personal belongings, flood insurance also plays a vital role in enabling recovery and return to normalcy after a disaster. Without it, homeowners may have to rely on federal disaster assistance, which is limited and often comes in the form of low-interest loans that must be repaid. Grants, when available, are usually modest and do not come close to covering the full cost of repairs or replacement.

Having flood insurance also allows policyholders to comply with local and federal regulations. Properties located in special flood hazard areas (SFHAs) with federally backed mortgages are required to carry flood insurance. Failure to maintain coverage can result in noncompliance penalties, forced placement of more expensive policies by lenders, and complications in securing or renewing mortgages.

THE ROLE OF FLOOD INSURANCE IN PROPERTY VALUE AND MARKETABILITY

Beyond immediate protection, flood insurance can affect a property's long-term value and marketability. In regions where flood risk is rising, homes that are insured against such risks are more attractive to buyers and investors. Prospective buyers are increasingly savvy about climate risks and often inquire about flood history, insurance coverage, and mitigation measures.

Moreover, homes that have previously suffered flood damage and were not insured may be stigmatized, facing reduced market value and greater difficulty in resale. On the other hand, properties with existing flood insurance policies and documented mitigation efforts, such as elevation above BFE, installation of sump pumps, or use of waterproof building materials, tend to command higher prices and sell more quickly.

Real estate professionals can help clients by encouraging them to request a Comprehensive Loss Underwriting Exchange (CLUE) report, which reveals any prior insurance claims on the property, including those related to flooding. Transparency around flood risk and coverage can facilitate informed decisions and foster trust between buyers and sellers.

COMMUNITY-LEVEL BENEFITS OF FLOOD INSURANCE PROGRAMS

While flood insurance is often viewed as an individual responsibility, it also has broader societal benefits. Communities that participate in the NFIP must adopt floodplain-management regulations designed to reduce future flood damage. These measures may include restrictions on development in floodways, elevation requirements for new construction, and stormwater management protocols.

In addition, the NFIP's CRS rewards participating municipalities for implementing best practices in floodplain management. Communities that go beyond the NFIP's minimum standards by enhancing public information, maintaining drainage systems, and preserving open space in floodplains earn CRS points that translate into discounted flood insurance premiums for their residents. This creates a powerful incentive for local governments to invest in resilience and engage their citizens in flood preparedness.

Flood insurance is not merely a bureaucratic requirement or optional add-on, it is a crucial safeguard against the financial and emotional consequences of flooding. As extreme weather becomes more common and flood zones shift due to urbanization and climate change, understanding the limitations of standard homeowner's insurance and the benefits of dedicated flood coverage is more important than ever.

Whether you live in a coastal city, a riverfront suburb, or an inland community that has never experienced significant flooding, the risk is real and often underestimated. Proactive steps, such as evaluating flood maps, consulting with insurance professionals, and securing appropriate coverage, can make the difference between recovery and ruin.

TYPES OF FLOOD INSURANCE

As homeowners, renters, and prospective buyers consider how to protect their properties from the ever-growing threat of flooding, it is critical to understand the types of flood insurance available in the United States. Choosing the right policy involves evaluating the differences between federally backed programs like the National Flood Insurance Program and private market options. Each type of flood insurance comes with its own advantages, limitations, and requirements, and the optimal choice often depends on a property's location, risk profile, and the owner's financial goals. This chapter delves into the distinctions between the NFIP and private flood insurance, explores building and contents coverage options, and examines regional variations in flood insurance offerings.

NATIONAL FLOOD INSURANCE PROGRAM

The primary source of flood insurance in the US is the National Flood Insurance Program (NFIP), administered by the Federal Emergency Management Agency (FEMA). It provides coverage for property and contents to homeowners, renters, and businesses in participating communities that adopt and enforce floodplain management regulations. NFIP policies cover up to $250,000 for residential buildings and $500,000 for commercial structures, with additional coverage available for contents (up to $100,000 for residential, $500,000 for commercial). Premiums are based on factors like flood zone, building age, elevation, and mitigation measures.

PRIVATE FLOOD INSURANCE

Private flood insurance has gained traction in recent years as a flexible alternative to NFIP coverage. These policies are issued by private insurers and are not bound by FEMA's pricing or coverage restrictions. As a result, private policies may offer higher coverage limits, faster underwriting, and additional protections, such as ALE, business interruption insurance, and replacement cost valuation for personal property. Some providers even offer optional riders to cover landscaping damage, basements, and detached structures more comprehensively.

Private flood insurance policies are typically customized based on risk assessments, property characteristics, and historical flood data. They are more likely to be used by owners of high-value homes or commercial properties, especially in areas where NFIP limits are insufficient. Some private insurers also offer "excess flood insurance," which supplements an existing NFIP policy to provide additional coverage above the program's caps. These excess policies are especially important for owners of luxury properties or businesses with expensive equipment.

PROS AND CONS OF EACH OPTION

The National Flood Insurance Program offers several important benefits. One major advantage is guaranteed availability and renewability. Once a property owner has an NFIP policy, FEMA guarantees that the coverage can be renewed annually, even if a major flood has occurred. This is especially important in maintaining continuous protection for properties in high-risk zones. Furthermore, NFIP coverage is federally backed, providing a level of financial security and reliability that many homeowners value. It is also often the only form of flood insurance accepted by lenders for properties located in SFHAs with federally backed mortgages.

That said, NFIP policies have notable limitations. The most obvious are the coverage caps of $250,000 for buildings and $100,000 for contents, which may not be sufficient for many homeowners. In addition, NFIP policies do not include ALE, which means that homeowners displaced by a flood may need to secure temporary housing out of pocket or through other insurance. The standardized policy format also means there is limited flexibility in coverage terms, which may not align with every homeowner's specific needs.

Private flood insurance policies, in contrast, offer a more personalized and often more comprehensive alternative. These policies can provide higher limits for both building and contents coverage, which can sometimes extend to millions of dollars. Private carriers may also include ALE and additional endorsements, such as sewer backup coverage and landscaping protection. The ability to tailor a policy to specific risks and preferences is a compelling feature for many policyholders.

Private flood insurance comes with its own set of challenges. It can be more expensive for properties in high-risk areas, as premiums are closely tied to individual property risk assessments. It is not available in all states or for all properties, with fewer providers offering policies in rural or historically flood-prone regions. Additionally, private insurers may choose not to renew policies after significant flood events, potentially leaving property owners without coverage when they need it most. While the NFIP guarantees policy renewals and is backed by the federal government, private carriers are profit-driven and may reassess risk more aggressively, sometimes raising premiums significantly after a single claim.

BUILDING COVERAGE VS. CONTENTS COVERAGE

Flood insurance policies typically consist of two components: building coverage and contents coverage. These can be purchased together or separately, depending on your needs.

Building coverage is essential for homeowners and property investors. It insures the structural components of a home, including the foundation, walls, floors, ceilings, electrical and plumbing systems, HVAC systems, built-in appliances, and cabinetry. In addition to the primary residence, NFIP building coverage includes up to 10 percent of the policy value for detached garages. Private insurers often expand this to include other detached structures, such as guesthouses, sheds, or pool houses.

Contents coverage, on the other hand, protects personal belongings within the insured structure. These items include furniture, clothing, electronics, small appliances, curtains, rugs, and portable units like window AC systems. Under the NFIP, contents are insured on an actual cash value (ACV) basis, meaning that depreciation is factored into the payout. Private insurers, however, frequently offer the option for replacement cost value (RCV) coverage, which reimburses the full cost of replacing items at current market prices without considering depreciation.

For renters, contents-only flood insurance policies are available, offering affordable protection for personal belongings. These policies are particularly useful for residents of high-rise apartments or multiunit dwellings where the building itself is insured by the property owner or condo association, but personal belongings remain vulnerable to flood damage.

REGIONAL VARIATIONS IN FLOOD INSURANCE AVAILABILITY AND POLICY TYPES

Flood insurance offerings can vary significantly across the United States based on state regulations, local risk assessments, and participation in federal or private programs.

Due to vulnerability to hurricanes and coastal flooding, Florida offers a robust private flood insurance market. Several domestic insurers operate in the state, offering comprehensive flood insurance policies that compete with NFIP coverage. State legislation passed in 2014 facilitated the growth of this market by removing regulatory hurdles for private carriers and encouraging innovative policy offerings. Florida's Office of Insurance Regulation actively monitors and promotes the expansion of the private market, making it one of the most competitive states for flood insurance.

Louisiana, particularly the New Orleans area, has long been associated with flood risk. NFIP coverage remains dominant, partly due to the legacy of Hurricane Katrina and subsequent federal investment in flood mitigation. While private insurance is becoming more common, many homeowners continue to rely on the federal program due to familiarity and access. The state has also implemented education initiatives to increase awareness of flood risk beyond traditional high-hazard zones.

In California, although commonly associated with earthquakes and wildfires, flooding is a growing concern, especially due to heavy rainfall, snowmelt, and wildfire-induced mudflows. While NFIP is the main provider, private insurers are gaining a foothold, particularly in urban areas like Los Angeles and San Francisco. California also has unique requirements for insurance disclosures during real estate transactions, requiring sellers to inform buyers of known flood hazards, which increases awareness and demand for flood insurance.

In the Midwest and Northeast, flood insurance uptake is generally lower, despite the increasing frequency of riverine and flash flooding. States like Illinois, Michigan, and New York have been affected by extreme weather events, including the remnants of Hurricane Ida in 2021, which caused severe flooding in parts of New Jersey and New York City. These events have prompted renewed calls for residents to consider flood insurance, even in non-coastal regions.

Each state maintains its own insurance regulatory authority, influencing which private insurers can operate and what policy types are available. For example, the New York Department of Financial Services and the California Department of Insurance both require that flood insurance policies meet specific consumer protection standards, including clarity of coverage terms and fair claims practices.

Local governments also play a crucial role. Communities that participate in the NFIP's Community Rating System program can earn premium discounts for residents by implementing and maintaining effective floodplain management practices. Depending on a community's CRS classification, discounts can range from 5 percent to 45 percent, significantly lowering the cost of NFIP premiums for residents.

The decision between an NFIP policy and a private alternative should be informed by an evaluation of coverage needs, property value, local availability, and long-term insurability. For many homeowners, especially those in high-risk or coastal areas, a combination of NFIP and private excess coverage may provide the most comprehensive protection.

Flood insurance is more than a regulatory checkbox; it is a lifeline that can determine whether a family can rebuild their home and life after a disaster. As climate change accelerates the frequency and severity of flooding across the country, proactive risk management through informed insurance decisions is more important than ever.

READ AND UNDERSTAND YOUR FLOOD INSURANCE POLICY

Understanding a flood insurance policy in full detail is a vital tool in safeguarding your property, finances, and peace of mind.

A flood insurance policy is more than a legal document; it's a roadmap for recovery. By understanding its terms, conditions, limits, and exclusions, as well as knowing about policy exclusions, deductible structures, and claim procedures, you can protect yourself from devastating losses and make smart financial decisions in advance of disaster. For example, some policyholders may not realize that flood insurance policies typically have a waiting period before becoming active. If a flood occurs shortly before the policy's 30-day waiting period ends, homeowners may be left without coverage altogether.

Take the time to read your policy thoroughly, ask questions, and seek professional guidance if needed. The better you understand your flood insurance coverage today, the more secure you'll be tomorrow.

WHY IT'S CRITICAL

Flooding is the most expensive natural disaster in the United States, causing billions of dollars in damage annually. While many homeowners secure flood insurance to meet basic legal or lender requirements, too few take the time to fully understand their coverage. This oversight often leads to devastating surprises when a flood hits. Too often, policyholders only discover what their flood insurance doesn't cover after they've experienced a loss. For instance, rising waters from a heavy rainstorm or river overflow may be covered, but flooding caused by a sump pump failure or sewer backup is typically excluded from most policies. Homeowners who live in flood-prone areas should ask about additional coverage options that address such exclusions.

After catastrophic floods, such as those caused by Hurricanes Katrina, Sandy, Harvey, and Ian, thousands of homeowners found themselves underinsured or completely ineligible for the full reimbursement they anticipated. In many of these instances, the aftermath was compounded by confusion regarding the claims process. Some homeowners were surprised to learn that their flood insurance did not cover certain types of damage, while others had misunderstood the terms and limits of their policy. They ignorantly believed they were fully protected when in reality, they had much less coverage than needed.

THE RISK OF UNDERINSURANCE

Underinsurance can occur when the coverage limits of a flood insurance policy do not fully align with the replacement cost of the property or belongings. The issue is compounded by a common misconception that flood insurance is meant to cover everything. In reality, many policies have specific coverage caps for different aspects of a property, such as the structure or contents, which may not account for inflation, improvements made to the home, or the current market value of personal property.

For example, if a homeowner buys an NFIP policy with a $250,000 limit for building coverage, but their home's actual replacement cost is $400,000 due to rising construction costs, the homeowner will face a significant shortfall in the event of a total loss. Similarly, while contents coverage under the NFIP may seem adequate with a $100,000 cap, homeowners with valuable personal items such as antiques, jewelry, or electronics may find that their policy falls far short of covering those items at their replacement value.

REAL-WORLD EXAMPLES OF UNDERINSURANCE

These are some high-profile disasters that illustrate the effects of underinsurance.

HURRICANE KATRINA

Perhaps one of the most tragic examples of underinsurance occurred in the aftermath of Hurricane Katrina. Thousands of homeowners in New Orleans believed they were fully covered for flood damage, only to find out that certain types of damage (like flood damage in basements) were excluded under their policies. Additionally, many had purchased minimal coverage and had not taken into account the high replacement costs of their homes, leading to significant financial losses. The event underscored the importance of having enough coverage to rebuild, not just repair. Many homeowners were forced to rely on FEMA assistance and loans, which were often insufficient and did not fully cover their losses.

HURRICANE SANDY

In New Jersey, New York, and surrounding states, homeowners who lived near the coastline or in flood-prone areas experienced massive damage. However, many were shocked to find that their flood insurance policies did not cover losses to things like outdoor structures, personal property in basements, or the deficit in business income for commercial property owners. One New Jersey family, for example, found their vacation home damaged beyond repair, but their insurance only covered a fraction of the replacement cost because their home was underinsured by at least 40 percent. This left them to grapple with substantial out-of-pocket expenses in addition to the emotional toll of losing their second home.

HURRICANE HARVEY

In Houston, Texas, the devastation from Hurricane Harvey left many homeowners reeling, particularly in areas where such catastrophic flooding is unprecedented. Many people who had been living in the area for years and had flood insurance were not fully aware of the coverage limits of their policies. For instance, in areas where the floodwaters reached higher-than-expected levels, some homeowners found that their NFIP policies did not cover all of their possessions, especially expensive items like furniture and electronics. Furthermore, with the scale of the disaster, many insurance adjusters were overwhelmed, and it took months for some homeowners to receive payouts, delaying their ability to rebuild.

HURRICANE IAN

One of the more recent flood disasters, Hurricane Ian devastated parts of Florida in 2022. In areas such as Fort Myers and Naples, many homeowners were left in shock when their flood insurance claims didn't cover the full extent of their losses. Some didn't realize that their flood policies had high deductibles or that certain flood-related damages, such as those caused by rising floodwaters after prolonged rain, weren't included. In some cases, insurance providers either underpaid claims or rejected them outright, citing issues with the type of damage being considered "flood-related" or failing to meet certain criteria. Residents also discovered that secondary coverage for personal property was often insufficient, especially when factoring in items that were stored in basements or garages.

TAKING ACTION: HOW TO AVOID THE PITFALLS

The takeaway from these real-world examples is clear: Homeowners and renters alike must actively engage in understanding their flood insurance policy. While some parts of a policy may be straightforward, others may require careful scrutiny. To ensure you're adequately covered:

1. **REVIEW YOUR POLICY ANNUALLY:** Flood insurance isn't a "set it and forget it" expense. Every year, take the time to review your coverage limits and assess whether they are still appropriate. As your home's value increases or you acquire more valuable belongings, it may be necessary to adjust your coverage to reflect these changes.

2. **CONSIDER ADDITIONAL COVERAGE:** Many policies, particularly through the NFIP, have significant gaps in coverage. Talk to your insurance agent about add-ons or endorsements that can extend your protection. For example, consider adding coverage for contents in a basement, or purchasing additional living expenses coverage if you live in a high-risk flood zone.

3. **ENSURE PROPER DOCUMENTATION:** Keep an up-to-date inventory of your belongings. Take photos and keep receipts for high-value items, so you can prove the value of your possessions if needed. This will help if you need to make a claim for personal property.

4. **UNDERSTAND EXCLUSIONS AND DEDUCTIBLES:** Read your policy closely to understand the exclusions, such as damage caused by landslides or mudslides, and review the deductible structure. In high-risk areas, deductible amounts can be quite high, and understanding this up front can help you prepare for potential out-of-pocket costs.

5. **STAY INFORMED ABOUT POLICY CHANGES:** Policies can change due to shifting flood risks, new exclusions, or changes in government regulations. Stay updated on these changes, particularly if you're in a flood zone that may be newly mapped or reclassified.

THE DECLARATIONS PAGE: YOUR POLICY AT A GLANCE

Every flood insurance policy begins with a declarations page, often referred to as the "dec page." This section acts as a summary of the policy's most critical information. It includes:

- The name of the policyholder
- The insured property's address
- The policy number
- Effective and expiration dates
- The amount of building and contents coverage
- Deductible amounts
- The name of the insurance company
- The premium paid

You should review the declarations page annually to confirm that all information is accurate and that coverage levels reflect any recent property improvements or major purchases.

KEY TERMS AND CLAUSES TO UNDERSTAND

Insurance policies are full of specialized terminology. While some terms may be familiar, others can be misleading or counterintuitive. Below are a few of the most important:

DEDUCTIBLES: This is the amount you must pay out of pocket before the insurance coverage begins to reimburse you. NFIP policies often have separate deductibles for building and contents, and higher deductibles typically result in lower premiums. However, be cautious: If your deductibles are too high, it may defeat the purpose of having insurance.

LIMITS OF LIABILITY: This refers to the maximum amount the insurer will pay for a covered loss. NFIP building coverage maxes out at $250,000, and contents at $100,000. If your home's replacement cost exceeds this, you may need supplemental coverage through a private insurer.

EXCLUSIONS: These are situations or items not covered by the policy. Understanding exclusions is just as important as understanding coverage. We'll explore this in more detail under What Flood Insurance Does Not Cover.

PROOF OF LOSS: A signed statement listing the amount you're claiming for flood damage. Under NFIP, this must typically be submitted within 60 days of the flood event.

WHAT IS COVERED BY FLOOD INSURANCE

Understanding what your policy does cover is essential. For NFIP policies, the two main components are building coverage and contents coverage.

BUILDING COVERAGE

This protects the physical structure of your home and integral components such as:

- The foundation, walls, and roof
- Plumbing and electrical systems
- Central air conditioning, furnaces, and water heaters
- Permanently installed cabinets, paneling, and bookcases
- Built-in appliances like dishwashers and stoves
- Detached garages (limited to 10 percent of building coverage)

CONTENTS COVERAGE

This protects personal belongings within the insured building. This typically includes:

- Furniture and electronics
- Clothing and appliances
- Curtains, portable air conditioners, and food freezers
- Valuables like artwork (up to set limits)

Contents coverage under the NFIP is optional, and many homeowners choose not to purchase it to lower premiums. They often regret this decision after a loss.

WHAT FLOOD INSURANCE DOES NOT COVER

Flood insurance is not a catch-all. There are many exclusions that homeowners frequently misunderstand:

ADDITIONAL LIVING EXPENSES: Most NFIP policies do not reimburse for hotel stays or temporary housing if your home becomes uninhabitable. Some private policies may offer ALE, but this should not be assumed.

BASEMENT IMPROVEMENTS: Finished basements, carpeting, paneling, and personal belongings stored in basements are generally not covered. Only essential equipment like furnaces and circuit breakers may qualify.

MOLD, MILDEW, AND MOISTURE: If mold is deemed preventable, your claim could be denied. Timely mitigation is crucial.

LOSS OF USE OR BUSINESS INCOME: These financial impacts are excluded in standard NFIP policies, though private insurers sometimes offer this protection.

VEHICLES, FENCES, AND LANDSCAPING: Automobiles must be insured through a separate auto policy. Likewise, external items like fences, pools, decks, and outdoor furniture are excluded.

REPLACEMENT COST VS. ACTUAL CASH VALUE

Understanding how payouts are calculated is another critical piece of the puzzle.

REPLACEMENT COST VALUE: This is the amount it would take to rebuild or replace your home or belongings with materials of similar kind and quality. NFIP offers RCV for building coverage under specific conditions: Mainly, that the home is your primary residence and insured to at least 80 percent of replacement cost or the maximum NFIP limit.

ACTUAL CASH VALUE: This deducts for depreciation. This is how most contents claims are paid. For example, a 10-year-old couch may cost $2,000 to replace but be valued at only $300 in a claim. Private insurers may offer RCV for contents, which is especially valuable for those with newer furnishings or electronics.

CALCULATING THE RIGHT COVERAGE: FOR STRUCTURE AND BELONGINGS

To ensure you're adequately protected, you need to estimate:

The Replacement Cost of Your Home

This is not the same as market value. Use tools like the Insurance Information Institute's rebuilding cost calculator or consult with a licensed contractor for a more accurate quote. Factor in:

- Square footage
- Construction type (wood, brick, etc.)
- Custom features (cabinets, countertops)
- Labor and material costs in your area

If your home's replacement cost exceeds the NFIP building limit of $250,000, consider private or excess flood insurance.

The Value of Your Personal Belongings

Conduct a home inventory. Document each item with:

- Description and estimated value
- Receipts or proof of purchase
- Photos or videos

Apps like Sortly or Encircle simplify this process and can be helpful in expediting claims.

UNDERSTANDING ENDORSEMENTS AND EXCESS POLICIES

Some private flood insurers offer endorsements or riders that expand coverage. These might include:

- Additional living expenses
- Basement improvements
- Business interruption
- Sewer backup and sump pump failure

HIGHLIGHT YOUR DEDUCTIBLE

One of the most important aspects of any insurance policy is understanding how much financial responsibility you bear in the event of a loss. The deductible is the amount you must pay out of pocket before the insurer begins covering your damages. In flood insurance, deductibles typically apply separately to building and contents coverage. For example, you may have a $2,000 deductible for the structure and a $1,000 deductible for personal belongings.

Tip: Use a highlighter or digital annotation tool to clearly mark your deductibles and limits on both building and contents coverage sections of the policy. Consider whether those amounts realistically reflect your potential loss and risk tolerance.

MARK ANY EXCLUSIONS THAT APPLY TO YOUR SITUATION

Flood insurance policies come with a range of exclusions that can dramatically affect your coverage. Common exclusions include damage caused by earth movement (such as landslides), mold and mildew not caused by the covered flood, and damage to items stored in basements. Finished basements are a particularly tricky area, as NFIP policies typically do not cover flooring, wall finishes, or personal belongings located in a basement, even if those items are lost due to flooding.

If you live in a coastal zone, be aware of any windstorm exclusions or requirements that pertain specifically to hurricane-related flooding. In areas impacted by hurricanes, such as parts of Florida and Texas, many policies differentiate between wind-driven rain and storm surge. Only the latter is typically covered by flood insurance; damage caused by rain entering through a broken window may be covered only under homeowner's insurance (and sometimes not at all, if a deductible is unmet).

Tip: Carefully review the Exclusions section of your policy and flag anything that may pertain to your property's layout, features, or location. If you have a finished basement, expensive landscaping, or storage below ground level, you'll want to know exactly what is and isn't covered. Based on those findings, consider alternative plans to protect those assets.

LOOK AT THE DEFINITIONS SECTION TO UNDERSTAND KEY TERMS

Insurance policies are legal documents, and the language they use is often highly specific. Misunderstanding a single term can spell the difference between a successful and a denied claim. For example, the NFIP defines "flood" as "a general and temporary condition of partial or complete inundation of two or more acres of normally dry land area or of two or more properties." This definition excludes water damage that affects only your property unless a neighboring property is also affected, which may surprise many homeowners.

Terms like "direct physical loss" also carry specific implications. "Direct physical loss" may exclude indirect damage, such as power outages that result in spoiled food, unless otherwise stated.

Tip: Read the definitions section slowly and carefully. Use sticky notes, margin annotations, or highlight tools to note how key terms are defined. When in doubt, contact your insurance agent or provider for clarification. A few minutes spent asking the right questions can save you thousands in denied claims later.

SAVE A DIGITAL AND PHYSICAL COPY OF YOUR POLICY IN A SAFE, ACCESSIBLE LOCATION

In the immediate aftermath of a flood, chaos and confusion often reign. Access to your policy (especially the declarations page, which outlines your coverage amounts, deductible, and insurer contact information) can make the difference between a smooth claims process and prolonged delays.

While it's important to keep a printed copy of your policy in a waterproof and fireproof container in your home, having a digital backup is equally crucial. Scan the policy and store it in a cloud-based account (such as Google Drive or Dropbox) or on an encrypted USB flash drive stored off-site. You should also email a copy to yourself and any family members involved in your financial or emergency planning.

Tip: During your annual insurance review (or at least once a year), update both your paper and digital records to reflect any policy changes. If you make upgrades to your home, such as installing flood vents, elevating utilities, or reinforcing foundations, notify your insurer and ensure the changes are reflected in your coverage.

STATE AND REGIONAL VARIATIONS

While the NFIP operates under federal guidelines, state regulations and private market offerings can affect your options. For example:

- In Florida, a growing number of private companies offer policies with broader coverage than NFIP.
- In California, wildfire-related mudslides can be covered as flood events under certain conditions.
- In Louisiana, where NFIP participation is high, the state also promotes mitigation credits to lower premiums.
- In Texas, some policies offer enhanced protection for oilfield equipment and agricultural structures.

Always check with your state's insurance department or a licensed agent about available options and regulations in your area.

FILING A CLAIM AFTER A FLOOD

Flood damage claims can be complex, and ensuring that the process goes smoothly is crucial to receiving the financial assistance necessary to recover. A successful claim hinges on understanding the steps required, properly documenting the damage, and adhering to specific insurance procedures. This section outlines the steps to take after a flood to ensure a successful claim and the best practices for documenting damage and keeping detailed records.

STEPS TO ENSURE A SUCCESSFUL CLAIM

The first priority after any flood event is ensuring the safety of yourself and your family. Ensure that the area is secure and that there is no immediate risk of additional flooding or hazards like electrical outages or gas leaks. Only once you are certain that it is safe to reenter your home should you begin to assess the damage.

In many cases, local authorities or emergency management agencies will issue warnings regarding whether it is safe to return to your property. It is crucial to follow these instructions, as reentering a property too soon can result in injury or death. If the floodwaters have not yet receded, it's also important to contact your flood insurance provider as soon as possible and report the loss.

NOTIFY YOUR INSURANCE COMPANY IMMEDIATELY

Once it is safe to do so, the next critical step is to notify your flood insurance provider. Under the terms of most policies, you must report flood damage to your insurer promptly, often within 24 to 48 hours of the event. Many insurance companies provide emergency services or flood claims assistance. Failure to report the damage in a timely manner could result in delays or even denial of the claim.

It's essential to provide your insurer with the necessary information, including the location of your property, a description of the damage, and any immediate actions you've taken to mitigate further loss (such as moving personal belongings to higher ground or using sandbags to prevent additional water from entering your home). Most insurance companies will send an adjuster to inspect the damage, so be prepared to schedule an appointment for this assessment as soon as possible.

TAKE EMERGENCY MEASURES TO PREVENT FURTHER DAMAGE

It's critical to take immediate action to prevent additional damage to the property. This includes actions like removing waterlogged furniture, securing valuables, and stopping the flow of water (if possible). Many insurance policies require homeowners to take reasonable steps to limit further damage after the flood. Failure to do so could result in a reduced claim payout or a denial of coverage.

However, be sure to document every step you take to demonstrate that you did everything within your control to minimize the impact of the disaster. This could include taking photographs of the property before and after you begin emergency actions such as moving furniture out of the flooded area or laying down tarps to protect floors.

PREVENT FUTURE DAMAGE AND HAZARDOUS CONDITIONS

Floodwaters often leave behind not only visible destruction but also unseen hazards. Once the water has receded, homeowners should assess their property for structural issues, mold growth, or other potential long-term damage. While waiting for the adjuster to arrive, it is essential to take preventive measures to avoid these issues from worsening.

Be sure to clean up any water as quickly as possible, especially from surfaces that may encourage mold or mildew growth, such as carpets, rugs, and walls. Mold can begin to form within 24 to 48 hours of water exposure, so timely action is critical. If the damage includes electrical equipment, it's best to have a licensed electrician inspect the property before reactivating any electrical systems.

WORK WITH THE INSURANCE ADJUSTER

Your insurance provider will likely send an adjuster to inspect the damage. The adjuster's role is to evaluate the extent of the destruction and determine how much compensation you are entitled to under your policy. This is a critical step in the claims process, and it's important to be present when the adjuster arrives so that you can ensure they have a clear understanding of the full extent of the damage.

It is essential to provide the adjuster with all the relevant information (see Document the Damage and Keep Records for guidance in this area).

Many homeowners find it helpful to have an independent contractor or professional on hand to discuss the damage and provide an estimate. This can help ensure that the adjuster's evaluation aligns with the reality of the damage, and it can be useful for negotiating a fair claim settlement.

DOCUMENT THE DAMAGE AND KEEP RECORDS

The key to a successful flood insurance claim lies in proper documentation. When disaster strikes, it's easy to feel overwhelmed by the sheer volume of tasks, but taking the time to thoroughly document all aspects of the damage can make a significant difference in the settlement process. Insurance companies typically require detailed records of the damage before they approve a claim, so keeping organized records is critical.

PHOTOGRAPHS AND VIDEOS: Photographic evidence is one of the most effective ways to document damage. Take clear and detailed photos of the damage to both the exterior and interior of your property. Don't just capture wide shots of the overall damage; focus on specific areas, like damaged furniture, ruined appliances, or warped walls. It's also important to photograph any personal items that were destroyed, particularly valuable ones like electronics, jewelry, or artwork.

INVENTORY LISTS: Create a list of all damaged or destroyed items in your home. This should include furniture, electronics, clothing, and any items of significant value. For each item, note the make, model, and year of purchase, as well as its original cost. If possible, include receipts or proof of purchase. The more detailed your inventory list, the better your chances of receiving compensation for the full value of your damaged property.

WRITTEN STATEMENTS: Keep a written record of the flood event itself, including the date, time, and severity of the flood. Record any conversations you have with your insurance company, adjusters, contractors, and others involved in the claims process. This will help you track progress and ensure that all important details are addressed.

PROFESSIONAL ESTIMATES: As previously mentioned, professional estimates can provide the insurance adjuster with a more accurate understanding of the cost to rebuild, which can influence the amount of compensation you receive. These professionals can also assess damage to elements like plumbing, HVAC, or electrical systems, which might not be immediately visible but can pose long-term risks.

KEEP RECORDS DURING THE CLAIMS PROCESS

It's essential to maintain organized records throughout the claims process to ensure that no information gets lost or overlooked. This includes keeping track of:

- **Communication Logs:** Log all communication with your insurance provider, adjusters, contractors, and any other relevant parties. Include dates, times, and a brief summary of each conversation.
- **Receipts for Temporary Housing and Emergency Repairs:** If your flood insurance policy includes coverage for additional living expenses, keep receipts for temporary housing, food, and emergency repairs. This will ensure that you are reimbursed for any costs you incur while waiting for your home to be repaired or rebuilt.

- **Claim Status Updates:** Stay in regular contact with your insurance company and monitor the status of your claim. If you receive a settlement offer or any communication regarding the claim, make sure to record it for future reference.

STAY PERSISTENT AND FOLLOW UP

Once the claim has been filed and the adjuster has assessed the damage, it's crucial to stay proactive. Claims can take time to process, especially after large-scale floods when insurers may be dealing with an influx of claims. However, it's important to follow up regularly to ensure that your claim is being processed in a timely manner.

If you feel that your claim is being delayed or underpaid, don't hesitate to ask for clarification or request a reevaluation. In some cases, hiring an independent adjuster to review the damage or negotiating with your insurance provider may be necessary to achieve a fair settlement.

Filing a flood insurance claim is a critical step in recovering from flood damage, but the process can be intricate and time-consuming. Remember, the key to a successful claim is proactive engagement: Stay organized immediately after the flood, keep meticulous records, and maintain open communication with your insurer. Through thorough preparation and persistence, you can navigate the claims process more smoothly and ensure a quicker, more efficient recovery and restoration of your property and belongings.

CHAPTER 3

UTILIZING NOAA FLOOD MAPS AND OTHER RESOURCES

Understanding and surviving floods involves much more than reacting to weather alerts or rising water levels. It requires a proactive approach rooted in accurate, timely, and scientifically grounded information. In the United States, one of the most critical resources available to both the public and emergency planners is the suite of flood maps and related tools developed by the National Oceanic and Atmospheric Administration. These maps provide essential data on flood risk, allowing individuals, communities, and policymakers to make informed decisions that can save lives and protect property.

One of the most significant benefits of NOAA flood mapping is its integration of real-time data with historical records. This allows users to distinguish between minor, moderate, and major flood events. AHPS, in particular, compiles precipitation data, streamflow observations, snowpack conditions, and soil moisture to generate dynamic flood forecasts. These maps are critical during severe weather events, such as hurricanes and heavy rainstorms, when quick access to accurate data can differentiate between evacuation and entrapment.

WHAT IS THE NOAA?

The National Oceanic and Atmospheric Administration, commonly referred to as NOAA, is a scientific agency within the United States Department of Commerce. Established in 1970, NOAA's mission is to understand and predict changes in climate, weather, oceans, and coasts, and to conserve and manage coastal and marine ecosystems and resources.

NOAA is a multifaceted organization, encompassing a number of line offices, including the National Weather Service (NWS), the National Ocean Service, the National Environmental Satellite, Data, and Information Service, and the Office of Oceanic and Atmospheric Research. These branches work together to monitor environmental conditions, issue warnings for severe weather, conduct environmental research, and manage the nation's marine resources.

Among its many responsibilities, NOAA plays a central role in flood monitoring and prediction. The agency provides real-time weather alerts, operates river forecasting centers, and produces vital flood-risk assessments. A cornerstone of its flood-risk communication is its flood-mapping initiatives, which allow citizens, governments, insurers, and builders to visualize and understand flood vulnerabilities on a local and national scale.

WHAT ARE NOAA FLOOD MAPS?

NOAA flood maps are detailed cartographic products designed to show areas at risk of flooding due to rainfall, river overflow, coastal surge, and sea level rise. These maps are tools for both planning and response. They are used by emergency managers preparing for hurricanes, homeowners considering insurance, and city planners deciding where to build infrastructure.

These maps do not stand alone. They are part of a larger ecosystem of flood-risk communication that includes data from FEMA, the United States Geological Survey (USGS), and the US Army Corps of Engineers. However, NOAA's maps are unique in that they often include dynamic, forecast-based elements and integrate real-time data into risk models.

Some of the key flood-mapping products and tools NOAA provides include:

- The **NOAA Flood Inundation Mapping Program**, which offers high-resolution, community-level inundation maps based on forecasted or observed river levels.
- **Sea Level Rise Map Viewer**, which displays how various scenarios of sea level rise could affect coastal areas.
- **Digital Coast**, a NOAA initiative providing data, tools, and training to support coastal management professionals.
- **Storm Surge Mapper**, which visualizes storm surge hazards during hurricanes

NOAA also contributes to FEMA's Flood Insurance Rate Maps (FIRMs), which are used to determine flood insurance requirements and guide local land use policies. Although FEMA is the lead agency for FIRMs, NOAA provides essential hydrologic, hydraulic, and meteorological data that underpin their accuracy.

HOW NOAA FLOOD MAPS ARE CREATED AND UPDATED

Creating flood maps that are accurate, reliable, and useful involves a complex interplay of data collection, modeling, and geographic information system (GIS) technology. These maps are not static; they evolve with new data, changing environmental conditions, and improved modeling techniques.

1. DATA COLLECTION

The creation of NOAA flood maps begins with a robust foundation of observational data. NOAA gathers data from the following network of sources:

- **River and Stream Gauges:** Operated by the USGS in collaboration with NOAA's National Weather Service, these gauges measure water levels and streamflow.

- **Radar and Satellite Systems:** These systems capture precipitation data, snowpack, and other hydrometeorological variables essential to understanding runoff and water accumulation.
- **Tide Gauges and Coastal Sensors:** For coastal flooding, NOAA maintains extensive tide gauge stations that measure sea level, tides, and storm surges.
- **Historical Flood Records:** Past flood events are crucial for establishing recurrence intervals and for calibrating hydrologic models.

This real-world data is continuously fed into NOAA's models to provide the most up-to-date and realistic representations of flood risk.

2. HYDROLOGIC AND HYDRAULIC MODELING

Once the raw data is collected, NOAA experts apply advanced hydrologic and hydraulic models to simulate how water flows through river basins, across floodplains, and along coastlines.

Hydrologic modeling calculates the amount of runoff generated by rainfall or snowmelt. It accounts for factors such as land cover, soil type, and topography. This modeling helps determine how much water enters a river or stream during a given storm.

Hydraulic modeling then simulates how that water moves through the environment. It considers the shape and structure of rivers, the location of levees or dams, and urban infrastructure such as culverts and storm drains. Together, these models can forecast how water will spread across the land, and which areas will be inundated.

3. GEOGRAPHIC INFORMATION SYSTEM INTEGRATION

With hydrologic and hydraulic models in place, NOAA uses GIS technology to create detailed flood maps. GIS enables the layering of flood-risk data over aerial imagery, political boundaries, and infrastructure maps.

Using GIS, NOAA can produce maps that show not just where flooding may occur, but also which roads, buildings, or facilities might be affected. This makes the maps invaluable for emergency planning and real-time decision-making.

For example, NOAA's Flood Inundation Mapping Program provides dynamic maps for 60 percent of the US, showing river flood extents at various forecast stages. These maps are integrated with NWS river forecasts, allowing users to see what areas are likely to flood in the coming days based on projected rainfall and river levels.

4. UPDATING AND VALIDATING MAPS

Flood risks are not static. As urban areas grow, rivers are redirected, levees are built or deteriorate, climate patterns shift, and flood vulnerabilities change. NOAA recognizes this and continuously updates its flood-mapping products.

Updates occur in several ways:

- **Post-Event Assessments:** After major floods, such as Hurricane Harvey or the Midwest floods of 2019, NOAA has conducted detailed studies to understand what happened and why. This often leads to revisions in flood models and maps.
- **New Data Inputs:** As more precise elevation data becomes available (e.g., via Light Detection and Ranging, or LIDAR), maps are refined to reflect updated terrain conditions.
- **Community Feedback:** Local governments and emergency managers often provide input or request map updates to reflect recent changes in land use or infrastructure.
- **Routine Model Improvements:** Advances in computing and modeling science are incorporated as part of NOAA's commitment to scientific rigor.

It's important to note that while NOAA maps are frequently updated, some maps such as FEMA's FIRMs may lag due to the time-intensive federal review process. NOAA's dynamic mapping tools help bridge this gap by providing near real-time updates for flood prediction and response.

THE VALUE OF NOAA FLOOD MAPS TO THE PUBLIC

NOAA flood maps are not just tools for academics or emergency planners, they are essential resources for homeowners, business owners, and communities.

These maps can guide your decisions about where to buy property, whether to purchase flood insurance, and how to prepare a flood emergency plan. In coastal areas, NOAA's sea level rise maps are instrumental in helping residents understand the long-term risks associated with climate change.

For example, in Miami-Dade County, Florida (a region highly vulnerable to sea level rise and storm surge), NOAA's tools have been used by city planners and residents alike to plan zoning, elevate buildings, and determine evacuation zones. In the wake of Hurricane Sandy, NOAA flood maps helped with rebuilding efforts in parts of New York and New Jersey, ensuring that new structures were more resilient to future events.

For local and state governments, NOAA's flood data aids in designing infrastructure, crafting emergency response plans, and applying for federal disaster mitigation funds. Schools, hospitals, and emergency shelters can be relocated from high-risk areas using these maps.

Insurers and lenders also use flood maps to assess risk and underwrite policies. Although FEMA's FIRMs are the legal standard for insurance decisions under the National Flood Insurance Program, NOAA's tools provide a more nuanced, real-time picture of flood potential that complements static maps.

LIMITATIONS AND COMPLEMENTARY RESOURCES

While NOAA's flood maps are powerful, they may not capture all local variations. Flash flooding, for example, is notoriously difficult to predict, especially in small urban catchments.

Moreover, not all NOAA flood maps are comprehensive. Some communities may not yet have detailed flood-inundation maps, or may lack high-resolution LIDAR terrain data needed for accurate modeling.

To overcome these gaps, users should consult complementary resources.

- **FEMA's Map Service Center:** For legal flood zones and insurance purposes.
- **USGS Streamgages:** For river level data.
- **State and local GIS offices:** Many states have their own flood risk tools.
- **The National Water Model:** A NOAA initiative to forecast water flow across 2.7 million stream reaches nationwide.
- **Community Flood Warning Systems:** Local governments often operate alert systems that integrate NOAA data with localized sensors.

HOW TO ACCESS AND READ NOAA FLOOD MAPS

For flood preparedness to be truly effective, knowing that flood maps exist is only the beginning. The real power lies in knowing how to access and interpret them. The National Oceanic and Atmospheric Administration (NOAA) offers several mapping tools and platforms that present flood risk information in a user-friendly and scientifically grounded way. However, for the uninitiated, these maps can appear complex.

This section serves as a practical guide to locating and navigating NOAA's flood maps, understanding the key elements on them, particularly flood zones, risk designations, and base flood elevation, and translating that information into actionable insights for safety, insurance, and planning.

STEP 1: IDENTIFY THE RIGHT NOAA MAP FOR YOUR PURPOSE

- For river flooding forecasts and real-time inundation mapping, use the Advanced Hydrologic Prediction Service (AHPS).
- For coastal surge risk, use the National Storm Surge Hazard Maps during hurricane season.
- For sea level rise and long-term coastal change, use the Sea Level Rise Viewer hosted on NOAA's Digital Coast platform.
- For general elevation and floodplain data, use NOAA's Coastal Flood Exposure Mapper.

Each tool serves a distinct purpose, so the first step is aligning your goal (e.g., understanding storm surge vs. river flooding) with the appropriate tool.

STEP 2: NAVIGATE TO NOAA'S MAPPING PORTALS

Here are some core URLs (or search phrases) to begin with:

- https://water.weather.gov/ahps, AHPS river forecasts and inundation mapping
- https://coast.noaa.gov/slr, Sea Level Rise Viewer
- https://coast.noaa.gov/floodexposure, Coastal Flood Exposure Mapper
- https://www.nhc.noaa.gov/nationalsurge, Storm Surge Hazard Maps

Search engines can also direct you to these resources as well. Try "NOAA AHPS flood map + [your town, zip code, or county]."

STEP 3: ENTER YOUR LOCATION

Most NOAA map platforms offer a search bar where you can enter your zip code, city, or coordinates. In AHPS, once you search your location, you'll be directed to the nearest river gauge site or forecast point. For example, entering "Cedar Rapids, IA" will take you to a local river forecast center showing river stage forecasts, observed levels, and corresponding flood thresholds.

The Sea Level Rise Viewer provides a visual interface where you can zoom in on coastal areas and explore the effects of different sea level rise scenarios (1 to 10 feet) on a map overlain with satellite imagery.

STEP 4: VIEW FLOOD MAP LAYERS

Once your location is selected, activate relevant layers, such as:

- Inundation boundaries
- 100-year floodplain
- Base flood elevations (where available)
- Critical infrastructure (hospitals, emergency services, etc.)
- Population and socioeconomic overlays (Digital Coast tools)

INTERPRETING FLOOD ZONES, RISK LEVELS, AND MAP INFORMATION

Flood maps often contain technical designations, color-coding, and overlays that can be intimidating. Understanding what these designations mean is crucial for determining your risk and making informed decisions about safety and insurance.

UNDERSTANDING FLOOD ZONES

Flood zones define areas based on the likelihood of flooding in a given year. These zones are defined by FEMA but appear in NOAA-related planning and tools to align communication. Here are the most common flood zone designations:

- **Zone A:** Areas with a 1 percent annual chance of flooding (also called the "100-year floodplain"). No base flood elevations are shown.
- **Zone AE:** Same risk as Zone A but includes base flood elevation data.
- **Zone V:** Coastal areas subject to storm wave action, also with a 1 percent annual flood risk. These are high-hazard zones.
- **Zone X (shaded):** Areas of moderate flood risk (0.2 percent annual chance of flooding, or "500-year floodplain").
- **Zone X (unshaded):** Areas outside mapped flood risk zones; they are minimal flood hazard, but not no risk.

RISK LEVELS AND PROBABILITIES

The "100-year floodplain" does not mean a flood happens once every 100 years. Rather, it indicates a 1 percent chance of a flood occurring in any given year. Similarly, a 500-year floodplain has a 0.2 percent annual chance.

These probabilities can be misunderstood. Multiple "100-year" floods can occur in close succession, as happened in Houston, Texas, which experienced major floods in 2015, 2016, and during Hurricane Harvey in 2017, all of which met or exceeded the "100-year" threshold. This illustrates the importance of using flood maps for trend and exposure analysis, not prediction.

DETERMINING YOUR BFE

BFEs are derived from hydraulic and hydrologic modeling and take into account:

- Topography
- Rainfall patterns
- Soil infiltration
- Land use (urban vs. rural)
- Flow dynamics in rivers and streams

When FEMA creates Flood Insurance Studies (FIS), they use this data to calculate BFEs, which then appear on FIRMs and may be referenced in NOAA inundation models.

THE ROLE OF BFE IN BUILDING AND INSURANCE

BFE has profound implications for:

- **Building Codes:** Local jurisdictions often require new structures in flood-prone areas to be built at or above BFE, often with additional freeboard (e.g., +one or +two feet) to provide a safety margin.
- **Insurance Premiums:** Properties below BFE typically face higher premiums, as they are statistically more vulnerable to damage.
- **Mitigation Planning:** Knowing a property's elevation relative to BFE helps owners decide whether to elevate structures, add flood vents, or relocate utilities.

As an example, post-Katrina rebuilding in New Orleans mandated that homes be elevated to at least BFE + three feet. This not only reduced future risks but also made structures eligible for lower insurance rates.

PUTTING IT ALL TOGETHER: A CASE EXAMPLE

Consider a homeowner in Wilmington, North Carolina, a coastal area prone to both river flooding and storm surge. Using the NOAA Sea Level Rise Viewer, they observe that a three-foot rise in sea level would inundate the low-lying portions of their neighborhood. Switching to the AHPS site, they check the Cape Fear River's latest flood forecasts and see projected crests based on upstream rainfall.

From the AHPS flood map, the homeowner learns their street lies within Zone AE, with a BFE of 12 feet. Upon reviewing a recent elevation certificate, they find their home's lowest floor is at 10 feet. This two-foot deficit increases both their risk and insurance costs.

With this information, the homeowner considers raising their structure, investing in flood-proofing improvements, or purchasing flood insurance at the actuarial rate. They also discuss evacuation planning with their family, now better understanding that their home is in a high-risk zone.

TIPS FOR EFFECTIVE USE OF NOAA MAPS

1. Cross-Reference with FEMA FIRMs: NOAA maps provide dynamic data; FEMA maps provide regulatory standards. Use both together for a comprehensive view.

2. Consult Local Floodplain Administrators: Your local emergency management office can help interpret maps and provide elevation certificates or community-specific overlays.

3. Use NOAA Maps During Active Weather: When flooding is imminent, NOAA's maps update in near real-time, offering crucial insight for decision-making.

4. Stay Updated: Flood maps change. Subscribe to NOAA alerts and watch for FEMA map updates in your region, especially after major development or disaster events.

For instance, during Hurricane Harvey in 2017, which inundated parts of southeastern Texas with over 50 inches of rain, NOAA's real-time flood mapping was crucial in managing emergency response operations. Local emergency managers used NOAA's tools to anticipate river cresting and identify neighborhoods at the highest risk. Similarly, in the 2019 Midwest floods, NOAA's predictive tools enabled farmers and municipal planners to gauge long-term impacts on agricultural fields and municipal infrastructure.

It is important for residents in flood-prone regions to familiarize themselves with NOAA's flood forecasting tools and integrate them into their preparedness routines. This includes monitoring flood watches and warnings issued by the NWS, subscribing to alert systems, and using interactive maps to evaluate flood risk before storms occur.

FEMA'S FLOOD MAP SERVICE CENTER: UNDERSTANDING YOUR FLOOD ZONE

While NOAA provides real-time and predictive flood data, the Federal Emergency Management Agency (FEMA) is responsible for producing and updating the official Flood Insurance Rate Maps (FIRMs) used by insurance companies, real estate professionals, and local governments. Again, these maps are available through FEMA's Flood Map Service Center (MSC) and are foundational to understanding long-term flood risk and regulatory requirements.

VIEWING THE MAP

Once you've entered your location and selected a corresponding map, the map viewer's interactive features allow you to zoom, identify flood zones, view parcel overlays, and download the FIRM as a PDF. Important data points include:

- Flood zone (e.g., Zone AE)
- BFE
- Map panel number and date
- Legend explaining symbols and lines

You may also access historical maps and preliminary (draft) maps, which are released during the remapping process before becoming official.

OTHER KEY FEATURES OF THE MSC

- **FIRMette Tool:** This feature allows you to create a printable, scaled portion of the flood map that includes the title block and legend, which is useful for permit applications or insurance documentation.
- **Letters of Map Change:** These include Letters of Map Amendment (LOMA) and Letters of Map Revision, which modify FEMA maps based

on new data or development. For example, if you elevate a home above the BFE, you may be eligible for a LOMA, removing your property from the floodplain. This could potentially reduce insurance costs.

- **Flood Insurance Study Reports:** These technical documents accompany FIRMs and explain the hydrologic and hydraulic data behind flood boundaries and BFEs. Engineers, surveyors, and developers often consult these for detailed planning.

LIMITATIONS AND IMPORTANCE OF UPDATES

It's important to recognize that FIRMs are static and can become outdated as land development, climate change, and hydrological patterns evolve. For example, after Hurricane Katrina in 2005, FEMA undertook extensive map revisions across Louisiana and Mississippi, as previously designated zones failed to reflect actual flood behavior. Residents whose homes had not previously been in a designated flood zone found themselves devastated by floodwaters and subsequently learned their insurance policies did not cover the damage.

Thus, while FEMA maps are authoritative, they must be used in conjunction with real-time data (such as NOAA's tools) and updated hazard modeling to obtain a comprehensive understanding of flood risks. Homeowners should check for preliminary flood maps released by FEMA, which indicate changes that will be incorporated into official maps following a public review period. Communities are encouraged to engage in this process through FEMA's Risk Mapping, Assessment, and Planning program.

LOCAL FLOODPLAIN ADMINISTRATORS AND PLANNING OFFICES

Most municipalities in flood-prone regions employ a floodplain administrator or have a designated official within the city planning department responsible for overseeing compliance with floodplain regulations. These professionals can provide property-specific information, including base flood elevation requirements, historical flood records, and building permit guidelines. They also serve as liaisons to FEMA and NOAA during the map revision process and are invaluable resources for interpreting how national maps apply at the parcel level.

Community members should establish a relationship with their local floodplain administrator, especially if they are considering buying, building, or significantly modifying a property in or near a flood zone. Engaging early in the planning process can prevent costly missteps and ensure that any construction meets flood-resilience standards.

Services often include:

- Reviewing building plans for flood compliance
- Issuing elevation certificates
- Advising on mitigation measures such as elevation or relocation
- Coordinating FEMA map updates
- Providing public education during flood awareness weeks or town hall meetings

LOCAL EMERGENCY MANAGEMENT AGENCIES (EMAs)

County and city emergency management agencies coordinate flood response and recovery efforts. These agencies often disseminate hyper-local flood information via social media, public alert systems, and community meetings. In areas like Houston, Miami, and Sacramento, each with unique flood vulnerabilities, local EMAs produce evacuation maps, shelter guides, and flood-survival tips tailored to regional hazards, including dam failure, urban flash flooding, and storm surge.

For instance, during the 2021 Tennessee floods, which killed over 20 people and destroyed hundreds of homes, local emergency managers were among the first to issue alerts and mobilize rescue efforts. Their knowledge of local terrain, drainage systems, and historical flood behavior was crucial in reaching vulnerable populations quickly.

Residents should register for their local emergency notification systems and participate in preparedness drills organized by EMAs. Doing so ensures they receive timely warnings and know what actions to take when flood threats arise.

PUBLIC WORKS AND WATER AUTHORITIES

In addition to emergency management agencies, local public works departments and water authorities manage stormwater infrastructure, levees, and retention basins. These entities can provide detailed insights into the engineering controls in place to mitigate flood risks. They often maintain stormwater maps, culvert maintenance schedules, and rainfall runoff models that are not available through federal databases.

Understanding how local stormwater systems function and their limitations can help homeowners and business owners better prepare for heavy rain events. For example, if a storm sewer system is undersized or clogged, flash flooding can occur even in areas outside the designated floodplain. Public works departments can also advise on mitigation grants or programs, such as FEMA's Hazard Mitigation Grant Program, that help residents fund floodproofing or elevation projects.

Most local government websites have a floodplain management or planning page. For example, the city of Austin, Texas, maintains a comprehensive floodplain information portal that includes mapping tools, development requirements, and educational videos.

COUNTY EMERGENCY MANAGEMENT

These departments are often the front lines during flood events and in disaster preparedness planning. They maintain:

- Flood siren systems and warning networks
- Evacuation routes and floodgate maps
- Sandbag distribution sites
- Storm drain and levee maintenance schedules
- Shelter and recovery center information

Local emergency management offices also coordinate with NOAA and FEMA during active weather events and disseminate localized flood alerts through systems like Nixle or Everbridge.

Case Example: In Houston's Harris County, the Harris County Flood Control District maintains its own advanced flood warning system, real-time rainfall data, and historical floodplain maps, offering a more detailed view than FEMA's FIRMs alone.

COOPERATIVE EXTENSION SERVICES AND CONSERVATION DISTRICTS

University extension programs and local conservation districts often partner with NOAA and FEMA to conduct flood-risk education. These groups provide:

- Community workshops on flood mitigation and insurance
- Rain garden and stormwater control education
- Grant assistance for resilience improvements
- Soil surveys and watershed models

For example, North Carolina State University's extension service has developed robust community outreach programs focused on stormwater management and rural flood risk education.

NEIGHBORHOOD ASSOCIATIONS AND GRASSROOTS NETWORKS

While government agencies, insurance providers, and emergency management systems form the backbone of large-scale flood response, local neighborhood associations and grassroots networks often serve as the first line of support before, during, and after a flood. These hyperlocal organizations play a vital role in bridging information gaps, mobilizing resources quickly, and reaching vulnerable populations that broader systems may overlook.

These groups are often composed of volunteers, civic leaders, and longtime residents, and they understand the unique challenges and geography of their neighborhoods. They can move more quickly than state or federal programs and often function with a level of trust and community buy-in that institutional actors cannot replicate.

COMMUNITY EMERGENCY RESPONSE TEAMS (CERTs)

CERTs are federally supported but locally implemented programs that train volunteers in disaster preparedness and response. Participants learn how to handle basic emergency functions such as light search and rescue, fire safety, and disaster medical operations.

In flood scenarios, CERTs may:

- Coordinate neighborhood evacuations.
- Check on elderly or disabled residents.
- Assist first responders with information gathering.
- Set up temporary community centers for supplies and updates.

After the 2013 Colorado floods devastated parts of Boulder County, local CERT volunteers played a pivotal role in evacuating residents, delivering sandbags, and organizing damage assessments in isolated mountain communities that emergency services couldn't immediately reach. Their prior training allowed them to act swiftly and effectively, reducing injury and confusion during the crisis. CERTs also excel in preparedness, often holding community meetings on flood planning, distributing checklists, or teaching residents how to shut off utilities before a storm.

FAITH-BASED EMERGENCY COORDINATION GROUPS

Churches, synagogues, mosques, and other faith-based organizations frequently act as logistical hubs during disasters. These groups are deeply embedded in communities, often with existing outreach programs to the homeless, low-income families, and elderly residents, demographics that are disproportionately impacted by flooding.

Faith-based groups may offer:

- Shelter and temporary housing.
- Donation and distribution centers for food, clothing, and toiletries.
- Emotional and spiritual support during displacement.
- Transportation assistance for evacuations or medical needs.

During Hurricane Harvey in 2017, Lakewood Church in Houston and other area churches served as vital shelters for thousands of evacuees. Smaller congregations across Texas and Louisiana also organized relief drives, sending truckloads of water, baby formula, and blankets into affected neighborhoods. These faith communities often maintain phone trees and social media networks that help disseminate real-time alerts more rapidly than official channels.

Furthermore, many faith-based organizations participate in interfaith coalitions that collaborate with FEMA and local government in long-term recovery planning, leveraging their trust-based relationships to deliver aid efficiently.

HOMEOWNERS ASSOCIATIONS AND NEIGHBORHOOD COUNCILS

While often known for managing landscaping or enforcing community rules, many homeowners associations (HOAs) play a significant role in flood preparedness and mitigation, especially in flood-prone developments. This is particularly true in master-planned communities or subdivisions located near retention ponds, levees, or creeks.

HOAs may:

- Maintain and inspect flood easements, stormwater drains, and detention basins.
- Contract private engineers for hydrological assessments.
- Distribute information on flood insurance and local regulations.
- Push for municipal improvements like upgraded drainage systems or floodplain mapping.

In Charlotte, North Carolina, several HOAs along Little Sugar Creek worked together to create a community stormwater watch group. They reported clogged storm drains to city officials, organized neighborhood clean-ups, and educated homeowners about installing rain gardens and pervious pavements. These local actions reduced the neighborhood's flooding severity during subsequent storm events.

In areas where municipalities are slow to act or underfunded, HOA-led efforts can fill critical gaps, preventing water buildup and protecting common areas from erosion and damage.

LOCAL ENVIRONMENTAL NONPROFITS AND ADVOCACY GROUPS

Environmental nonprofits, watershed alliances, and flood-resilience coalitions are often at the forefront of long-term, science-based flood-mitigation strategies. These groups work on both policy and practical implementation levels, often serving as liaisons between government, residents, and private industry.

Such organizations may:

- Advocate for wetland preservation and green infrastructure.
- Conduct floodplain education and mapping workshops.

- Monitor local water quality and streambank erosion.
- Coordinate volunteer efforts for tree planting and native vegetation projects.

The Coalition for the Upper South Platte (CUSP) in Colorado has been instrumental in restoring riparian zones following flood and wildfire damage. By planting native vegetation, reinforcing riverbanks, and removing invasive species, CUSP has helped reduce runoff speed and sediment buildup, thereby lowering flood risks.

In Louisiana, Bayou Rebirth, a grassroots nonprofit, works with New Orleans neighborhoods to build bioswales and rain gardens that absorb excess rainwater. Their efforts not only reduce localized flooding but also engage residents in understanding how everyday landscaping choices affect regional flood risk.

THE STRENGTHS OF GRASSROOTS NETWORKS

What distinguishes these community-based networks is not just their proximity to the problem but their flexibility, social trust, and human capital. These organizations are embedded in the rhythms of the neighborhood. They understand which residents need extra help, which streets flood first, and how to communicate effectively, whether through Facebook groups, WhatsApp, Nextdoor, or even door-to-door visits.

During the 2021 floods in Middle Tennessee, residents in the city of Waverly credited much of their survival and rapid response to a volunteer-led Facebook page that kept the community informed in real time. When power and cell service were out, ham radio operators and local churches stepped in to keep communication lines open.

These hyperlocal systems can also be lifesaving for non-English speakers, undocumented residents, or others who might not access official alerts due to language barriers, distrust, or technological gaps. For example, in parts of Houston and South Florida, bilingual volunteers from local mosques and cultural centers have provided real-time translations of emergency broadcasts, helping residents make critical evacuation decisions.

COLLABORATING RESOURCES FOR COMPREHENSIVE FLOOD PREPAREDNESS

Relying on a single source of flood information can leave individuals and communities exposed to unnecessary risk. Instead, effective flood preparedness requires synthesizing information from NOAA, FEMA, and local and community resources.

In many successful flood mitigation efforts, these resources are used in concert. For example, the city of Charlotte, North Carolina, has developed one of the most advanced integrated flood information systems in the country. By combining FEMA's maps with high-resolution local floodplain modeling and real-time NOAA data, Charlotte's flood-management team provides residents with street-level risk maps and alert systems that dramatically improve response time and public awareness.

CHAPTER 4

PREPARING YOUR HOME BEFORE A FLOOD OR HURRICANE

In an age of rapidly changing climate and increasingly frequent extreme weather events, safeguarding one's home against floods and hurricanes is no longer a concern reserved for those living in low-lying coastal areas. From the unprecedented flash floods in New York City in 2021 to the destruction caused by Hurricane Ian in Florida in 2022, communities across the United States and the globe are realizing that resilience begins at home.

FLOOD AND HURRICANE DEFENSES

Temporary flood defenses are often the first line of protection for homes facing an imminent storm. These solutions do not eliminate the risk of water intrusion entirely, but they can significantly reduce the volume and impact of incoming floodwaters.

Sandbags remain one of the most commonly used flood defenses, valued for their affordability, accessibility, and ease of deployment. Proper placement is crucial: sandbags should be laid in a staggered brickwork pattern with plastic sheeting behind them to improve water resistance.

However, sandbags have limitations. They are labor-intensive, degrade quickly, and provide only temporary protection. Additionally, after use, they must be disposed of properly to prevent environmental contamination from sewage-laden floodwaters.

In more advanced preparations, portable flood barriers such as modular aluminum panel systems or water-filled tubes (e.g., AquaDam or Tiger Dam) offer stronger, more reliable protection. These barriers are designed to withstand higher water pressure and can be rapidly deployed. For example, during the 2019 floods in the Midwest, portable water-filled dams were successfully used to protect critical infrastructure in towns along the Mississippi River, reducing economic losses.

Flood skirts and shields can be installed on doors, garages, and window wells, creating a watertight seal during a flood event. Unlike sandbags, which are passive and degrade with use, these mechanical solutions can be reused and integrated into a home's permanent design. Some modern systems even automatically deploy when triggered by sensors detecting rising water levels.

Municipalities also encourage residents to make use of stormwater diversion measures, such as trench drains, swales, and sump pumps, which help redirect water away from foundations. Regular maintenance of these systems (clearing gutters, ensuring drains are unobstructed, and checking backflow preventers) is as important as their installation. Failure in these systems can lead to structural flooding even if exterior defenses hold.

SECURING WINDOWS, DOORS, AND ROOF FROM WIND AND WATER DAMAGE

In addition to water, one of the most destructive aspects of a hurricane is the wind. Hurricane-force winds can turn everyday objects into projectiles, tear off roofing materials, and shatter windows, dramatically increasing the risk of water intrusion and structural failure.

Windows and doors are particularly vulnerable. Impact-resistant glass or storm shutters (accordion-style, Bahama, or roll-down models) are vital for homes in hurricane-prone areas. These systems are tested to withstand winds exceeding 130 mph and impacts from debris, standards outlined by the Florida Building Code and Miami-Dade County's high-velocity hurricane zone criteria. Shutters should be installed on all openings, including garage doors, which often fail under wind pressure and lead to catastrophic roof uplift.

Where storm shutters are not feasible, plywood boarding remains a reliable albeit labor-intensive option. Panels should be cut and labeled ahead of time to ensure rapid deployment. Predrilling holes and storing screws and tools nearby allows for quick boarding when time is limited.

Roof integrity is another crucial aspect of preparation. Roofs should be inspected annually for loose or damaged shingles, particularly in hurricane-prone regions. Homeowners should consider upgrading to hurricane straps or clips, which secure the roof trusses to the walls, preventing uplift during high-wind events. As a result of Hurricane Andrew (1992), these changes, which began with the 1994 South Florida Building Code and were later incorporated into the statewide Florida Building Code, for example, mandated a more resilient construction standard for new buildings and have become a national model for hurricane-prone areas.

Additionally, sealing the roof deck, a practice involving the application of waterproof tape or sealant over joints, can dramatically reduce water penetration in the event of shingle loss. Florida's "sealed roof deck" requirement has become a national best practice following research showing that even when shingles are lost, water intrusion can be minimized by 90 percent if the deck is sealed.

Exterior doors should be reinforced with three hinges and a deadbolt lock at least one inch long. Double doors (such as French doors) often need additional locking pins and brackets. Weather stripping should be inspected and replaced as needed to ensure watertight seals.

Finally, landscaping must not be overlooked. Trimming trees, removing dead branches, and securing outdoor furniture can prevent these objects from becoming airborne hazards.

ELEVATING UTILITIES AND VALUABLES ABOVE EXPECTED FLOOD LEVELS

Elevation is one of the most effective long-term strategies for flood mitigation. This principle applies not only to homes built on stilts or raised foundations, but also to utilities, appliances, and personal property within any structure.

Utilities such as electrical panels, HVAC systems, water heaters, and fuel tanks should be elevated above the base flood elevation. FEMA's *Homeowner's Guide to Retrofitting* offers detailed instructions on how to elevate or relocate mechanical systems either to a higher floor or to specially built platforms. During Hurricane Sandy in 2012, thousands of homes in New York and New Jersey suffered total loss of utilities due to ground-level installations. Those that had elevated systems, or whose utilities were located on higher floors, were able to return to service much faster.

Sump pumps and battery backup systems play a key role in managing interior water intrusion. It is essential to test these systems monthly and replace batteries every two to three years. A sump pump should be paired with a check valve to prevent backflow and ensure that expelled water does not return via drains or pipes. See page 86 for a more detailed discussion of sump pumps.

Backflow valves should be installed on all sewer lines to prevent floodwaters from causing sewage to back up into the home, a common and dangerous occurrence during floods. These devices are mandated in many urban areas but are often neglected in older properties.

For valuable personal property, homeowners should keep documents, electronics, and heirlooms in waterproof containers or safes. Items such as birth certificates, insurance policies, and passports should be digitized and stored securely online or off-site.

If feasible, homeowners should consider creating a "flood-safe zone," a second-story room or elevated area where important items and supplies can be relocated before a storm. Modular shelving and raised flooring can also be used in basements or ground floors to minimize contact with floodwater.

While no home can be rendered entirely immune to the forces of nature, the steps outlined in this chapter can dramatically improve a family's ability to withstand and recover from floods and hurricanes. Preparedness is not a one-time event but an ongoing process of planning, investing, maintaining, and learning from past disasters.

The examples from Hurricane Katrina, Hurricane Sandy, Hurricane Harvey, and countless others have taught us that proactive preparation often determines the line between survivable damage and catastrophic loss. Installing temporary barriers, securing the home's structural envelope, and elevating essential systems are not just acts of maintenance, they are acts of stewardship and responsibility.

EMERGENCY SUPPLIES AND FOOD

When facing a flood or hurricane, the window for action often closes quickly. Roads become impassable, supply chains grind to a halt, and emergency services can be overwhelmed or inaccessible. In such scenarios, the resources you have on hand become not just helpful but lifesaving. A well-prepared emergency supply cache transforms a household from vulnerable to resilient, ensuring that essential needs are met when infrastructure and outside help are compromised.

At the core of any emergency preparedness effort is a carefully assembled cache of essential supplies. FEMA recommends that households maintain enough provisions to support all members for a minimum of 72 hours. However, in areas with high flood risk or limited emergency infrastructure, a 7 to 10 day supply is more appropriate, especially considering the extended recovery periods observed during Hurricane Katrina, Hurricane Maria (2017), and Hurricane Ian.

Water is the most critical resource. FEMA advises storing one gallon per person per day, split between drinking and sanitation. For a family of four, a three-day minimum translates to 12 gallons; for 10 days, 40 gallons. Store water in sealed, food-grade containers and label with the date of storage.

Commercially bottled water is ideal, but water can also be safely stored for up to six months with unscented household bleach (eight drops per gallon).

In flood scenarios, tap water can become contaminated with sewage, chemicals, or runoff. Therefore, in addition to stored water, every emergency kit should include:

- Water purification tablets
- Portable water filters (e.g., LifeStraw, Sawyer Mini)
- Collapsible water containers to collect rainwater if necessary

Nonperishable, calorie-dense, and easy-to-prepare food items are ideal:

- Canned goods: beans, meats, vegetables, fruits
- Meal, Ready-to-Eat (MRE) packages
- Granola bars, trail mix, peanut butter
- Powdered milk or electrolyte drink mixes
- Baby formula and pet food, if applicable

Ensure that your food supply includes a manual can opener. Store food in a dry, elevated location, such as upper kitchen cabinets, to avoid contamination during flooding.

STORING YOUR EMERGENCY SUPPLIES

When preparing for a flood, it's not just the contents of your emergency kit that matter, it's *where* and *how* you store those supplies can make the difference between a smooth evacuation and a chaotic scramble. Unlike earthquakes or snowstorms, floods can render ground-level storage useless, contaminate drinking water, and increase the risk of infection through prolonged exposure to damp, unsanitary conditions. Tailoring your emergency kit to these risks is essential for safety and long-term resilience.

Flood-specific storage planning ensures that your efforts to be prepared won't be washed away when you need them most. Too many families have learned this the hard way, especially during historic flood events like the Midwest floods of 2019, where many survivors discovered their carefully assembled emergency kits had been completely submerged, contaminated, or swept away because they were stored in low-lying areas like basements or garages.

ELEVATION IS ESSENTIAL: Your emergency kit should never be stored on or near ground level in flood-prone areas. Ideally, place it on a second floor, in an attic, or on an elevated shelf well above anticipated flood levels. FEMA and emergency management agencies recommend keeping supplies at least two feet above the base flood elevation (BFE) for your area whenever possible. If your home is a single-story structure, look for high interior shelving or heavy-duty waterproof lockers that can float or remain sealed even if submerged.

WATERPROOFING IS EQUALLY CRITICAL: Store your supplies in large, durable plastic bins with gasket-sealed lids. These are readily available at hardware and home improvement stores and are often labeled for outdoor, marine, or tactical use. Some bins are even designed to lock or stack, adding another layer of security. For added protection, you can line the inside of your bins with heavy-duty trash bags or plastic sheeting, creating a double barrier against water intrusion. See additional information in Waterproof Containers and Protective Coverings on page 95.

REDUNDANCY IMPROVES RESILIENCE: It's wise to create multiple kits tailored to different scenarios:

- **Home Emergency Kit:** Your primary and most comprehensive kit should be stored in your house, containing essentials like food, water, medical supplies, flashlights, batteries, sanitation items, extra clothing, and important documents.
- **Car Kit:** A smaller version should be kept in your vehicle, containing basics like bottled water, snacks, a first-aid kit, a flashlight, a phone charger, and blankets. In the event you're caught away from home or must evacuate quickly, this kit is your mobile lifeline.
- **Go-Bag:** Every household member should have a personal go-bag, lightweight and ready to grab in seconds during a sudden evacuation. These bags should include basics like a water bottle, high-calorie snacks, medication, a copy of identification, emergency contact numbers, a flashlight

with spare batteries, an emergency whistle, a compact first-aid kit, and cash. A change of clothes and a lightweight rain poncho are also helpful. For children, include comfort items such as a favorite toy or blanket to help reduce anxiety. Go bags should be stored in elevated areas, such as near the garage or main exit or on shelves or wall hooks high enough to avoid floodwater contamination. Also see What to Take with You If You Must Leave Quickly on page 121.

Consider the climate and shelf life of stored supplies. In humid areas, moisture-absorbing silica gel packets can prevent mildew in containers. Rotate your stored food and water every six months and check expiration dates on medications, batteries, and packaged goods. Vacuum-sealing food or using Mylar bags with oxygen absorbers can extend the shelf life of dry staples like rice, beans, and pasta. For water storage, opt for BPA-free containers, and consider water purification tablets or portable filtration systems in case you need to use local sources.

Labeling and inventory tracking also help keep your supplies organized and ready. Use a waterproof marker or label maker to clearly identify the contents of each container. A printed inventory sheet taped inside the lid can help family members quickly locate items under stress. For digital backup, take photos of each kit and store them in a cloud drive accessible to all household members.

Special considerations for households with children, seniors, or pets:

- Include diapers, formula, and children's medications in kits for infants and toddlers.
- Pack extra glasses, hearing aid batteries, or mobility aids for elderly family members.
- Don't forget pet food, leashes, vaccination records, and collapsible bowls for your animals.

Finally, communicate your emergency kit locations with everyone in your household. Conduct a walkthrough during flood season, explaining how to access the kits, what's inside, and how to use essential tools like a flashlight, radio, or water filter. Even older children should know where to find and how to open the containers in case adults are not immediately available.

[Flood-Specific Gear: Floodwaters can rise quickly and carry contaminants, debris, and hidden dangers like sharp objects or live electrical wires. To stay safe during evacuation or clean-up, include practical tools and protective equipment. Chest waders or waterproof boots will allow you to navigate flooded areas without exposing your skin to harmful waterborne substances. Masks such as N95 or P100 respirators can be crucial in post-flood environments where mold and dust can become airborne health hazards. Plastic sheeting and duct tape can be used to create makeshift barriers or seal leaks temporarily, and headlamps will keep your hands free in the dark. A hand-crank or battery-operated weather radio is also essential for receiving NOAA weather updates and emergency instructions when power and internet are down.

OVERLOOKED ITEMS TO INCLUDE IN YOUR KIT: Some of the most overlooked but vital items in a flood emergency kit are lighting tools, waterproof clothing, backup power sources, and a comprehensive first-aid kit.

Lighting is critical during flood-related power outages. Choose long-lasting LED flashlights and store at least two in your home, along with plenty of extra batteries. Keep batteries in moisture-proof packaging. A hand-crank flashlight can serve as a reliable backup. Avoid candles altogether, as they pose a serious fire risk, especially in environments with possible gas leaks.

Protective clothing should include waterproof outer layers (jackets, pants, and ponchos) as well as rubber gloves for handling contaminated materials. Warm, moisture-wicking base layers help regulate body temperature and prevent hypothermia, even in warmer climates. During Hurricane Harvey, many stranded residents suffered from exposure and cold after prolonged time in wet clothes and stagnant water.

Power sources become lifelines in floods, especially when phone batteries die or electricity is out for days. Every adult should have access to a portable USB power bank. Solar-powered chargers are a good backup when gas-powered generators aren't available. Many modern hand-crank radios now come with built-in USB charging ports for phones and small devices; these can be a game-changer when communication infrastructure goes down.

FIRST-AID SUPPLIES FOR FLOOD CONDITIONS: In flood scenarios, minor injuries can escalate quickly. Dirty water and debris heighten the risk of infection, and limited access to professional medical care makes self-treatment necessary. A robust first-aid kit should go beyond Band-Aids and gauze. Include antiseptic wipes, alcohol pads, antibiotic ointment, and hydrocortisone cream to treat rashes and skin irritation caused by damp clothing or contaminated water. Antifungal powder is useful for preventing athlete's foot, especially when feet stay wet for extended periods. Oral rehydration salts can prevent dehydration from heat exposure or illness, and over-the-counter medications like pain relievers and antihistamines can help manage common ailments.

BASIC FIRST-AID KIT CONTENTS

A well-stocked kit includes:

- ❍ Antiseptic wipes
- ❍ Alcohol pads
- ❍ Antibiotic ointment (e.g., Neosporin)
- ❍ Sterile gauze and bandages
- ❍ Medical tape
- ❍ Tweezers and scissors
- ❍ Gloves (nitrile, non-latex)
- ❍ Pain relievers (acetaminophen, ibuprofen)
- ❍ Antihistamines
- ❍ Hydrocortisone cream
- ❍ Anti-fungal powder
- ❍ Oral rehydration salts

Households that rely on prescription medication, such as insulin, EpiPens, or inhalers, should maintain an emergency supply with clearly marked instructions. These should be stored in waterproof bags and checked regularly for expiration. As the CDC advises, keeping tetanus shots up to date is also vital, since flood environments often contain sharp debris that can cause dangerous puncture wounds.

MULTI-TOOLS AND EMERGENCY REPAIRS: A sturdy multi-tool is one of the most versatile additions to any emergency kit. Brands like Leatherman and Gerber offer models designed for survival and flood conditions. The best multi-tools include a knife, scissors, small saw, pliers, and screwdrivers. In an emergency, these tools can help you cut fabric or rope, open canned food, repair damaged gear, or even shut off gas or water mains. Some models also come equipped with seatbelt cutters and glass breakers, especially useful if you must evacuate a vehicle in high water.

Each household should also keep a standalone gas shutoff tool and an adjustable wrench near the home's main valve. This can prevent explosions or fires if your gas line becomes compromised. After events like Hurricane Katrina and the 1994 Northridge earthquake, delayed shutoff of gas supplies was a leading cause of post-disaster fires and injuries.

PSYCHOLOGICAL AND COMMUNICATION PREPAREDNESS

While much attention is placed on physical supplies during disaster preparation, the mental and emotional toll of flooding is often underestimated. Fear, isolation, and prolonged stress can impair judgment, delay response times, and increase trauma, especially in children and vulnerable adults. To help ease the psychological burden, it's important to include comfort items in your emergency kit.

INCLUDE GAMES, BOOKS, AND COMFORT ITEMS: Creating a sense of routine and calm in the midst of chaos can significantly improve resilience, especially for families with young children.

MAINTAIN A WRITTEN CONTACT LIST IN CASE PHONES ARE LOST OR DRAINED: Equally critical is planning for communication when digital networks fail. Keep a written contact list of key phone numbers in your emergency kit in case cell phones are lost, wet, or out of power. Establish a family communication plan. Establish a family communication plan well in advance and designate an out-of-town contact person who can coordinate updates, decide on two safe meeting locations (one near the home, one outside the neighborhood), and practice these protocols annually. A well-rehearsed communication plan reduces panic and confusion, ensuring that even in the most disorienting circumstances, your family has a roadmap to stay connected and make safe decisions.

In any emergency, the time to prepare is before the crisis begins. Floods and hurricanes are unpredictable in their path and magnitude, but your ability to respond should not be. Assembling and maintaining a robust, flood-focused emergency supply kit is one of the most tangible and empowering steps you can take to protect your household.

The destruction observed in places like New Orleans in 2005, Puerto Rico in 2017, and Kentucky in 2022 shows how quickly modern conveniences can disappear. For many survivors, the comfort available in the hours and days that followed these disasters was determined not by government response but by what they had prepared in advance. Emergency supplies are not simply a precaution, they are the foundation of your home's survival strategy. They buy time, preserve health, and offer peace of mind when it is needed most.

SUMP PUMPS AND BASEMENT FLOODING

Among the most vulnerable parts of any home during a flood is the basement. Even light rainfall in flood-prone areas can overwhelm drainage systems and seep through foundation walls. During heavier flooding or hurricanes, water accumulation in basements can become rapid and dangerous, not only structurally and financially but in terms of personal safety too.

WHAT IS A SUMP PUMP?

A sump pump is a mechanical device installed in a pit (called a "sump") at the lowest point of a basement or crawl space. Its purpose is to collect and expel water that infiltrates the area, pumping it away from the home to a designated drainage area. While many homes rely on electrically powered sump pumps, these become useless during a power outage, an extremely common occurrence during hurricanes or major storms. That's where battery-operated or water-powered backup sump pumps come into play.

BATTERY-POWERED PUMPS

The 2021 flash flooding in the New York Metro Area, caused by remnants of Hurricane Ida, led to thousands of flooded basements and several fatalities. In many cases, power had already failed by the time water levels rose, rendering electric pumps inoperable.

A battery-operated sump pump, installed alongside your primary pump, automatically activates when the main pump fails or if power is cut. High-capacity models can run for 8 to 24 hours continuously and are capable of removing thousands of gallons of water per hour.

Key Considerations

- **Battery type:** Choose a deep-cycle marine battery over standard car batteries for longer runtime and durability.
- **Maintenance:** Test monthly and replace the battery every three to five years.
- **Alarm systems:** Many models include a high-water alarm to alert you to pump failure or rising water levels.
- **Float switch:** Ensure the pump includes a float switch that triggers operation only when necessary.

WATER-POWERED PUMPS

These are powered by municipal water pressure, not electricity or batteries. While effective, they require a reliable water supply and are not ideal in drought-prone or rural areas. Check local plumbing codes before installation. Proper installation and regular testing are critical. Even a well-designed system can fail if not maintained.

LIFE VESTS AND FLOTATION DEVICES

Personal flotation is one of the most overlooked and misunderstood aspects of flood preparedness. Many flood-related deaths don't happen in deep water but in deceptively shallow, fast-moving currents. Just 6 to 12 inches of water can knock over an adult or sweep away a vehicle. Tragically, many victims drown while trying to walk or drive through flooded areas, believing the water is manageable. The simple act of wearing a life vest can spell the difference between life and death.

The US Coast Guard estimates that over 85 percent of flood-related drowning victims are swept away unexpectedly often while trying to flee rising water. In those moments, there's no time to search for gear or assemble a plan. A properly fitted, US Coast Guard–approved life vest (Type I, II, or III) becomes an immediate lifesaving measure. Yet many households don't include them in their emergency kits or fail to store them where they're easily accessible.

TYPES OF FLOTATION DEVICES

TYPE I (OFFSHORE LIFE JACKET)

Has the highest level of buoyancy and is made to keep or turn an unconscious person face-up in the water. Best for rough or open waters where rescue may be delayed.

TYPE II (NEAR-SHORE VEST)

Best for calm, inland waters where rescue will be quick. Slightly less buoyant than Type I but more comfortable.

TYPE III (FLOTATION AID)

Commonly used by recreational paddlers and rescue teams, this type offers comfort and ease of movement but is best suited for conscious users in known waters.

THROWABLE DEVICES (E.G., RING BUOYS, SEAT CUSHIONS)

These can be helpful for rescuing others but are not substitutes for wearing a life vest yourself.

WHEN TO WEAR A LIFE VEST DURING A FLOOD

If your home is flooding and you may need to evacuate through water. Here are situations when you should wear a life vest:

- When wading through any flooded area to reach higher ground.
- While assisting others through water, especially children, elderly, or nonswimmers.
- During rooftop or attic rescues while waiting for emergency responders.

To be effective, life vests must be:

- Sized correctly for each household member (including children).
- Stored in easy-to-reach places like entryways, hall closets, or second-floor supply kits.
- Brightly colored or equipped with reflective tape to increase visibility for rescuers.
- Checked annually for damage, buoyancy, and fit.

WHAT IF YOU DON'T HAVE A LIFE VEST OR FLOTATION DEVICE?

If you don't have commercial life vests, you can attempt to create a makeshift flotation device, though these should be treated as last resorts. Sealed plastic bottles tied together, foam couch cushions, or even inflatable pool toys can offer some buoyancy, but they are far less reliable and offer no guarantees. Investing in proper vests for each family member is always the safest choice.

CHILDREN, INFANTS, AND VULNERABLE ADULTS

Those at greater risk, such as young children, elderly individuals, or anyone with mobility limitations, require special planning and considerations. Children should have vests specifically rated for their weight and size. Infants need life vests with head support and flotation collars designed to keep their faces above water. These should be stored close to beds, cribs, or evacuation exits, ready to grab at a moment's notice.

By including flotation devices in your flood-preparedness strategy, you add a vital layer of protection. In an emergency, every second counts, and the right gear can save a life, perhaps your own or that of a loved one.

ROPE AND LADDERS: SECURING YOURSELF AND ASSISTING OTHERS

Floodwaters are deceptively dangerous. While they may appear calm or shallow, they often conceal strong currents, hidden debris, and shifting surfaces. You can be knocked off your feet in as little as six inches of moving water. In these chaotic conditions, having rope and ladders on hand can be life-saving. These simple tools can provide stability, facilitate rescue, and offer vital access points to safer ground.

ROPE: A MULTIPURPOSE LIFELINE

Rope can be used in several critical ways during a flood. One of the most practical applications is tying off for stability. If you need to cross water, a rope anchored to a sturdy object like a tree, utility pole, or structural column can serve as a lifeline, helping prevent falls or sudden sweeps downstream. This kind of setup, often called a safety line, provides a secure handhold and can help guide you safely through flowing water.

Ropes are also commonly used for rescue lines. If someone is stranded or unable to cross on their own, throwing them a rope gives them something to hold onto or allows you to pull them toward safety. In some cases, multiple ropes may be strung across areas to help groups cross together, one by one. Rope can also be used to secure property, such as tying down outdoor furniture, trash bins, propane tanks, or even tools and ladders, preventing them from floating away or becoming dangerous projectiles in high water.

When selecting rope for flood preparedness, polypropylene is a top choice for water use because it's lightweight and floats, ideal when visibility is low or the water is deep. Nylon rope is another excellent option due to its strength and slight elasticity, which makes it suitable for rescue efforts. The rope should be at least three-eighths of an inch in diameter to support a person's weight, and a length of 50 to 100 feet is typical for home emergency kits. For ease of use, store your rope in a dedicated rope bag with a carabiner attached for quick deployment. Always wear gloves when handling rope under load to prevent rope burns or hand injuries.

LADDERS: VERTICAL ESCAPE TOOLS

As floodwaters rise, families may find themselves trapped in low-lying areas, basements, or even on the first floor of their home. When the water comes faster than expected, moving upward to an attic or rooftop might be the only option. For this reason, portable ladders should be part of every flood preparedness plan, especially in homes without built-in escape routes.

Rope ladders are compact, lightweight, and can be rolled out from an upper window or balcony in seconds. They're particularly important for two-story homes, providing an escape route when stairs are submerged or unsafe. Telescoping ladders are another excellent option. These ladders collapse into a compact size for easy storage but can quickly extend to reach rooftops or upper-story windows. If you have an attic but no built-in access, installing an attic ladder or having a collapsible one nearby can turn that space into a viable emergency shelter.

To ensure their reliability, ladders should be:

- Stored on the upper floor of your home, not in the garage or basement, where floodwaters can render them inaccessible.
- Made of durable, water-resistant materials, such as aluminum or sealed hardwood, to withstand prolonged exposure to moisture.
- Rated to hold at least 250 pounds, allowing for safe use by adults, possibly while carrying children or supplies.

The importance of having an escape ladder was tragically underscored during Hurricane Harvey, when several people drowned after becoming trapped in attics without a way to reach the roof. In response to these incidents, FEMA now advises all homeowners in flood-prone areas to plan for roof access. In addition to a ladder, some homeowners choose to store an axe or hand saw in the attic to create an emergency exit through the roof if needed.

ADDITIONAL TIPS FOR ROPE AND LADDER USE DURING FLOODS

- ❍ Practice deploying your ladder and rope before an emergency, so you're confident using them under pressure.
- ❍ Label storage containers clearly, and include a headlamp or flashlight in your upper-floor emergency cache to make nighttime use easier.
- ❍ Check ropes and ladders annually for wear, rust, or fraying.

While general preparedness lays the foundation for flood safety, it is these specialized tools (sump pumps, life vests, ropes, and ladders) that provide the means to act swiftly and decisively in a flood emergency. These tools address the harsh realities of high water: that it compromises mobility, contaminates everything it touches, and can rise faster than anticipated.

MAINTENANCE AND TRAINING: ENSURING TOOLS ARE READY WHEN YOU NEED THEM

Emergency tools are only as effective as their condition and your ability to deploy them quickly under pressure. During a flood, even a few seconds of hesitation or a malfunctioning piece of gear can make the difference between a safe evacuation and a dangerous situation. That's why regular maintenance and hands-on training are just as important as acquiring the tools in the first place.

Start by conducting a biannual inventory check of your flood preparedness supplies. Set reminders at the start of hurricane season and again before winter storms to go through all emergency equipment. Check that rope isn't frayed, that batteries are still viable, that ladders deploy smoothly, and that plastic storage bins remain sealed and undamaged. Look for corrosion, mold, or any water damage, especially in gear stored for long periods. Rotate out expired items like medications, food, and batteries.

Equally important is practicing with your equipment. Being familiar with tools before an emergency strikes will reduce panic and improve response times. Practice deploying rope ladders from upper-story windows, securing rope safety lines around anchor points, and using sump pumps or water vacuums if you own them. Ensure each family member knows where key tools are stored and how to use them appropriately. Assign responsibilities: who handles the ladder, who gathers the emergency kits, who secures the pets. Practice scenarios like evacuating in the dark or simulating flooded entryways to build muscle memory and confidence.

If possible, take basic flood safety and rescue training. Organizations like the American Red Cross, FEMA, and many local fire departments offer community-based training on emergency response, including how to assist others safely. These sessions often include guidance on using flotation devices, helping vulnerable individuals, and basic first aid. For families with teens or older children, involving them in this training can be empowering and help build community resilience.

Use color-coded labels or reflective tape to make storage bins easily identifiable in low light. Label ropes, life vests, and flotation devices for individual users to avoid confusion during an evacuation. For example, label a child's life vest with their name, weight range, and a reflective sticker to make it easier to identify during rescue operations.

PROTECTING FURNITURE AND BELONGINGS—STRATEGIC SAFEGUARDS BEFORE THE FLOOD

Floods are among the most damaging and disruptive natural disasters, capable of washing away not just structures but the lives and memories contained within them. While much attention is understandably focused on evacuation plans, flood defenses, and life-saving measures, the protection of household belongings, such as furniture, valuables, family heirlooms, and essential documents, can significantly influence both recovery timelines and financial outcomes.

Begin by identifying high-value or irreplaceable items, such as:

- Family photo albums, legal documents, and passports
- Laptops, hard drives, and other electronics
- Jewelry and heirlooms
- Upholstered or wooden furniture
- Musical instruments or artwork

Create a written pre-flood plan that outlines which items should be moved and to where. This ensures efficient action under stress. Preparing your home in advance of a flood requires proactive effort. This section outlines methods for safeguarding your possessions.

RAISING FURNITURE AND VALUABLES TO SAFER GROUND

We've already discussed relocating high-value or irreplaceable belongings to a second story, attic, or overhead storage.

In single-story homes or homes without significant vertical space, the solution is to elevate objects using available means. Heavy-duty plastic or metal shelving units can lift items one to three feet off the ground, often enough to clear rising water in minor floods. Similarly, placing furniture atop cinder blocks or custom-built platforms can prevent damage. Major appliances such as washers, dryers, and HVAC units should also be elevated using custom platforms or makeshift risers, such as cinder blocks. According to FEMA guidelines, these should be raised at least one foot above the base flood elevation (BFE) to reduce the risk of water damage and ensure safe operation after the flood event.

The value of such precautions is vividly illustrated in disasters like Hurricane Katrina and the 2019 Midwestern floods, when floodwaters inundated tens of thousands of homes. In many cases, items stored just two or three feet above ground level remained untouched even when lower floors were submerged. These real-world outcomes underscore the importance of acting before water arrives. Once a flood warning is issued, there is often little time to safely relocate furniture or boxed valuables, so planning and executing such steps in advance is critical.

Don't overlook the garage and basement when preparing for a potential flood; these spaces are often the first to take on water during a flood event. Remove or relocate vulnerable and hazardous items. Move tools and power equipment to higher ground to prevent corrosion and electrical hazards. Relocate cans of paint, solvents, and other flammable materials, as they can leak during a flood and contaminate both your home and the surrounding environment. Lawn mowers and electrical garden tools are susceptible to water damage and pose safety risks if submerged. Additionally, securely store or move automotive supplies such as oil, antifreeze, and cleaning fluids, since they can create serious environmental hazards and complicate cleanup efforts if released into floodwaters. Properly securing or relocating these items in advance can significantly reduce loss and mitigate contamination risks.

WATERPROOF CONTAINERS AND PROTECTIVE COVERINGS

Physical elevation is not always possible, especially in crowded homes, apartments, or for large, immovable items. In these cases, containment becomes the next line of defense. Floodwater isn't just rain water or water from a river or ocean; it typically carries with it mud, sewage, chemicals, and debris. Anything it touches is at risk of becoming both contaminated and structurally damaged.

For small to medium items, waterproof storage containers offer an affordable and highly effective solution. Heavy-duty plastic storage bins with gasket-sealed lids are among the most reliable and cost-effective options. For added durability, look for bins specifically rated for outdoor or marine use, as they're designed to withstand water exposure. For smaller valuables, such as electronics, passports, or treasured family photos, dry bags are a great choice. Commonly used by hikers and boaters, these flexible, waterproof bags are lightweight, seal tightly, and are easy to store. Vacuum-sealed bags can also help protect against moisture and mold; however, they are not completely watertight when submerged, so they should always be placed inside another waterproof container for double protection.

Avoid using the following materials for flood preparation:

- Cardboard boxes, which easily disintegrate when wet
- Fabric bins, which absorb moisture and encourage mold
- Metal boxes without rubber seals, which can rust and leak

If you're unable to move heavy furniture, you can still take steps to waterproof it. Use thick plastic sheeting (six millimeters or thicker) to wrap large items like couches, beds, and shelving units. Make sure to secure the plastic with waterproof tape around all edges to prevent seepage. Elevate furniture using risers or cones, and place a layer of plastic between wood surfaces and risers to prevent water from wicking into the furniture. For wooden pieces, consider applying a water-resistant sealant to the legs and undersides. Placing aluminum foil or rubber pads under furniture legs can also provide a protective barrier against moisture absorption.

Electronics require special care. Always unplug devices, move them to higher ground, and cover them securely with plastic or place them in waterproof containers. Remove batteries to prevent corrosion, and label wires and cords for easy reconnection after the event.

Photographs, while often backed up digitally, should still be physically protected. Store original prints in acid-free, waterproof albums, and include desiccant packets to reduce humidity and mold growth inside the container. Taking these steps ahead of time ensures that your critical records and cherished memories are safe, even if your home is not.

For critical documents such as birth certificates, passports, medical records, insurance papers, or property deeds, combining digital redundancy with physical protection is essential. Documents should be scanned and stored in secure cloud storage as well as on an encrypted USB drive kept in a waterproof case. The originals can be placed in a zippered waterproof bag or a fireproof, waterproof safe, a small investment that can prevent enormous legal and financial headaches after a disaster.

APARTMENT LIVING: SHARED VULNERABILITIES AND STRATEGIC ADAPTATION

Living in a multiunit apartment or condominium presents unique challenges in flood preparation. On the surface, residents of higher floors may assume they are safe from rising water. Although a higher elevation offers natural protection, apartment dwellers are often just as vulnerable, but in different ways.

For one, critical building systems are usually located in basements or ground floors. Electrical transformers, boilers, HVAC units, and water pumps can all be disabled by flooding even when individual apartments are untouched. This can result in long-term outages, mold intrusion through shared ventilation systems, and unsafe conditions for days or even weeks following a storm.

Tenants living on the first or second floors should approach flood preparation much like homeowners. Furniture and valuables should be relocated to higher interior areas, while storage areas, particularly those in building basements, should be emptied of anything sensitive or irreplaceable. Items kept in communal storage lockers must be placed on shelves and sealed in waterproof containers, as basement flooding is one of the most common outcomes in urban flood events.

Tenants and building associations should communicate clearly before flood season. Inquire with property managers about flood insurance coverage, the location of emergency shutoffs, the condition of sump pumps, and any previous history of water intrusion. During Hurricane Sandy, many New York City apartment buildings lost power and water for days because of submerged basements and poorly coordinated emergency responses. Those with building-level flood planning fared far better in maintaining livable conditions and accessing necessary repairs.

It is also wise for apartment residents to keep personal flood kits at the ready, including portable lighting, copies of documents, basic food supplies, and portable battery banks, especially if upper floors must be accessed without elevators during a power outage.

PLANNING FOR RECOVERY: INVENTORY AND MOLD MITIGATION

Protecting belongings also involves preparing for what comes next. The recovery phase is often prolonged, emotionally draining, and logistically complex. However, smart planning before disaster strikes can ease the burden.

Homeowners and renters alike should keep an up-to-date inventory of all significant possessions. This can be as simple as taking dated photographs of each room and maintaining a written list with serial numbers and estimated values. Free inventory apps are available that allow users to upload images and store data securely online. This documentation is essential in the event of an insurance claim.

Finally, consider the risk of mold. Even items that appear undamaged can become hazardous within 48 hours if not properly dried. Any porous material that has come into contact with floodwater (cardboard, upholstered furniture, rugs, and books) is likely unsalvageable unless cleaned and dried professionally. To mitigate risk, use moisture absorbers such as silica packets or dehumidifiers in enclosed spaces, and ventilate flooded areas as soon as it is safe to do so.

Hard surfaces should be disinfected using a bleach solution (typically one cup of bleach to one gallon of water), followed by thorough drying. For sensitive materials like photographs or documents, immediate freezing can sometimes halt mold growth until professional restoration is available.

Protecting your belongings from a flood is not an act of anxiety, it is an investment in resilience. The damage from a flood extends far beyond wet floors and ruined drywall. It touches the tangible history of your life: the dining table passed down from your grandparents, your child's first drawings, the photographs of your wedding, and the electronics that connect you to the outside world.

Through proactive strategies you can drastically reduce the emotional and financial toll of a flood. What cannot be prevented entirely can be mitigated with care, planning, and early action.

As seen in historic floods from New Orleans to Houston to coastal Florida, the greatest losses are often preventable. By focusing not only on the structural defenses of your home, but also the preservation of your belongings, you move one step closer to true preparedness.

PROTECTING YOUR VEHICLE

Cars and trucks are highly vulnerable to flood and hurricane damage, often underestimated in comprehensive disaster preparation plans. A flood-damaged vehicle may become a total loss, even with minimal water exposure, and the financial impact can be substantial.

CHOOSE SAFE PARKING LOCATIONS: ELEVATION AND SHELTER

When flooding or hurricanes threaten, the location where your vehicle is parked can dramatically influence its fate. Floodwaters, especially flash floods, can rise rapidly and sweep vehicles away, while hurricanes bring not only water but also powerful winds and debris that can cause structural damage.

The fundamental principle is to park your vehicle as high and as sheltered as possible. Elevated areas such as hilltops or upper levels of parking structures are preferred because water tends to accumulate in low-lying zones first. Flood maps provided by local authorities or FEMA's flood risk data can help identify which areas are less prone to inundation.

Parking garages, particularly those on upper floors, offer considerable protection against floodwaters. They also provide shelter from wind-driven debris, hail, and falling branches common in hurricanes. However, it's essential to understand the specific garage's flood resilience, as many have ground-level entrances that can flood or fail during extreme weather.

Conversely, parking near rivers, drainage ditches, or coastal shorelines is inherently risky. Similarly, street parking, even on seemingly elevated streets, can be dangerous, as water can rise quickly and vehicles may become stranded or swept into deeper water. In many catastrophic floods, such as those experienced during Hurricane Harvey in 2017, thousands of vehicles were irreparably damaged simply because they were left parked in vulnerable zones.

If no elevated parking options are available, the best practice is to move your vehicle to a friend or family member's property located on higher ground. Early planning and arrangements can save thousands in repairs and the emotional toll of losing your vehicle.

PRECAUTIONARY STEPS: DISCONNECTING THE BATTERY AND COVERING THE VEHICLE

Beyond location, certain precautionary measures can reduce flood-related damage and facilitate quicker recovery. Disconnecting the battery is one such measure. Floodwaters can cause electrical shorts, damaging sensitive electronic systems and igniting fires. By disconnecting the battery prior to flooding, you reduce the risk of electrical damage and accidental ignition. It's important to note that modern vehicles often have complex computer systems, so disconnecting the battery should be done carefully, ideally by someone familiar with automotive electronics or under professional guidance.

Additionally, covering the vehicle with a waterproof tarp or specialized car cover can provide a barrier against rain, hail, and flying debris. While a cover cannot prevent floodwater intrusion, it can minimize superficial damage such as chipped paint or broken glass. Some specialized covers are designed to protect against UV rays and moisture, which may help if the vehicle must be stored outdoors for extended periods.

ADDITIONAL CONSIDERATIONS AND FINAL PREPARATIONS

Before floodwaters arrive, remove any personal belongings from your vehicle. Items like documents, electronics, and clothing can be damaged or lost during flooding. Also, fill the gas tank if time permits; a full tank prevents moisture buildup inside the fuel system and ensures the vehicle is ready for evacuation if necessary. Checking and topping off fluids and ensuring tires are properly inflated enhances vehicle readiness.

Equally important is documentation. Photographing the vehicle's condition before the storm provides a valuable record for insurance claims. Securing registration and insurance paperwork in waterproof cases ensures that critical information is accessible when needed most.

Lastly, establishing a clear evacuation plan for your vehicle is essential: knowing when and how to move it, and keeping ahead and informed of weather developments. Acting early can be the difference between saving your car and losing it to rising floodwaters.

After a flood, avoid starting a vehicle submerged in water, as this can cause catastrophic engine damage. Instead, have the car inspected by a qualified mechanic before attempting to operate it.

As with all flood preparedness measures, early planning and situational awareness are paramount. Recognizing the vulnerability of your vehicle and taking action well before disaster strikes is the best defense against the financial and emotional costs of flood-related vehicle loss.

VEHICLE FLOOD PREPAREDNESS CHECKLIST BEFORE A FLOOD OR HURRICANE

1. IDENTIFY SAFE PARKING LOCATIONS

❍ Locate elevated areas such as hills, upper floors of parking garages, or high ground away from flood-prone zones.

❍ Check local flood maps and warnings to understand risk levels.

❍ Arrange alternative parking at friends' or family's homes in safer locations if necessary.

2. PREPARE THE VEHICLE

- ❍ Remove all personal belongings, important documents, and valuables from the car.
- ❍ Fill the gas tank to avoid moisture buildup and ensure fuel is available if evacuation is needed.
- ❍ Check tire pressure and fluid levels to ensure the vehicle is ready for sudden use.

3. DISCONNECT THE BATTERY

- ❍ Carefully disconnect the battery to prevent electrical damage or fire during flooding. Seek professional help or consult your vehicle's manual for proper procedures.

4. COVER YOUR VEHICLE

- ❍ Use a waterproof tarp or a specialized car cover to protect the exterior from rain, hail, and debris.
- ❍ Secure the cover or tarp tightly to prevent it from potentially blowing away.

5. DOCUMENT YOUR VEHICLE

- ❍ Take photos of your car's condition before the storm for insurance purposes.
- ❍ Keep your vehicle registration and insurance information in a waterproof container.

6. PLAN FOR EVACUATION

- ❍ Know the routes to safe parking and have a plan for moving your vehicle quickly.
- ❍ Monitor weather updates and flood warnings to act in a timely manner.

POST-FLOOD VEHICLE INSPECTION GUIDE

If your vehicle has been exposed to floodwater:

1. Do Not Start the Engine

- Starting a flooded vehicle can cause severe engine damage, including hydrolock.
- Have the vehicle towed to a qualified mechanic for a thorough inspection.

2. Check for Visible Damage

- Inspect under the hood for water intrusion, mud, or debris.
- Look for water in the oil, transmission fluid, and brake fluid.
- Examine the interior for water damage, wet upholstery, and odors indicating mold.

3. Electrical Systems

- Test the lights, horn, power windows, and dashboard electronics once the vehicle is dry.
- Have the battery and electrical systems professionally evaluated.

4. Brakes and Tires

- Have brakes inspected for water damage and rust.
- Check tires for debris and damage, and ensure proper inflation.

5. Clean and Dry the Vehicle Thoroughly

- Remove all water and moisture from the interior immediately.
- Use fans and dehumidifiers to prevent mold growth.
- Clean and disinfect to reduce the risk of bacterial contamination.

6. Insurance Notification

- Report the flood exposure to your insurance company promptly.
- Provide pre- and post-flood photos and documentation for claims processing.

CHAPTER 5

WHAT TO DO DURING A FLOOD

Floods are among the most unpredictable and fast-moving natural disasters. Unlike hurricanes or snowstorms, which often provide days of warning, floods can develop and escalate within minutes. Triggered by intense rainfall, storm surges, or dam failures, floodwaters can turn familiar streets into dangerous rivers and transform a secure home into a life-threatening trap. In these moments, knowing what to do both physically and mentally direct you from catastrophe to survival.

Remaining composed under pressure is one of the most critical aspects of flood survival. Panic can cloud judgment and lead to risky or irrational decisions. Regulating stress in the moment is as essential as understanding how to reinforce a doorway or navigate an evacuation route. Simple breathing techniques and grounding strategies can help maintain mental clarity and improve responsiveness during emergencies.

Maintaining contact with family members, neighbors, and emergency services becomes vital when a flood strikes. Reliable communication tools, such as charged cell phones, battery-operated radios, and emergency apps, can provide crucial updates and serve as lifelines. When conventional networks fail, preestablished communication plans can make it easier to coordinate and seek help.

Flood responses vary depending on the situation, and knowing whether to evacuate or shelter in place is key. Evacuation requires clear decision-making, understanding local routes, packing efficiently, and traveling safely amid changing conditions. When sheltering in place, the challenge shifts to preserving clean water, staying warm, securing food, and protecting the home from further damage.

Power outages frequently accompany flood events, compounding the danger. Without electricity, homes lose lighting, heat, refrigeration, and communication capabilities. Safe generator use, resource conservation, and alternative lighting and heating methods become essential to ensure safety and comfort until conditions stabilize or assistance arrives.

Moving water poses one of the gravest dangers during a flood. Even shallow, fast-flowing water can carry away cars and knock you off your feet. Understanding how to avoid entering moving water and what to do if caught in it can save lives. Flotation devices, proper body positioning, and knowledge of how to use surrounding debris for survival can increase the odds of staying safe.

Vulnerable individuals often face the greatest risk. Children, the elderly, those with disabilities, and pets all require special considerations and tailored planning. From evacuation supplies to mobility equipment, thoughtful preparation ensures no one is left behind or exposed to unnecessary danger.

The emotional toll of a flood is also significant. Fear, confusion, and anxiety can impair decision-making and increase panic, especially in high-stress environments. When both you and your family or support network maintain calm and practice teamwork, you foster better outcomes during and after the disaster.

A well-informed and measured approach to floods can dramatically reduce harm and improve resilience. With the right knowledge, tools, and mental preparedness, it's possible to protect yourself and your loved ones even in the most challenging flood conditions.

STAYING SAFE AND CALM

An often-underestimated element in flood survival is the mental and emotional state of those caught in these crises. Staying safe during a flood requires more than knowledge of evacuation routes or waterproofing techniques; it demands composure and clarity of mind.

THE IMPORTANCE OF STAYING CALM: HOW PANIC CAN LEAD TO DANGEROUS DECISIONS

The human response to acute danger often triggers a survival mechanism colloquially known as the "fight-or-flight" response. In the context of floods, this can translate into impulsive actions such as rushing into floodwaters to rescue property, attempting to drive through submerged roads, or failing to heed evacuation warnings. All of these behaviors significantly increase risk. The 2015 flooding in South Carolina provides a stark example: Many casualties resulted not from the floodwaters themselves but from attempting to cross rapidly rising streams, underestimating water force. The National Weather Service and the American Red Cross both emphasize that "Turn Around, Don't Drown" is a critical mantra precisely because panic can cloud judgment and encourage hazardous decisions.

Panic typically stems from the body's acute stress reaction, which causes a surge in adrenaline, heightened heart rate, and rapid breathing. While this response is evolutionarily designed to prepare us for immediate threats, it can also impair cognitive functions such as rational thinking, memory recall, and decision-making. In flooding scenarios, where conditions are fluid and rapidly evolving, maintaining the ability to assess surroundings critically is paramount.

One psychological phenomenon to consider is "tunnel vision," which often accompanies panic. A panicked person may focus narrowly on escaping the immediate threat without awareness of safer options or secondary dangers. For example, during the catastrophic 2005 floods caused by Hurricane Katrina, many victims made impulsive attempts to reach rooftops without accounting for debris in the water or structural instability. Unfortunately, some drowned or suffered injuries as a result.

The danger of panic extends beyond the individual: It can trigger a chain reaction in families or communities. If a family member becomes frantic, others may be compelled to follow suit, leading to chaos and disorganized evacuations. Coordinated response efforts hinge on clear-headedness.

UNDERSTANDING THE PSYCHOLOGICAL IMPACT OF FLOODING

Flood events inflict not only physical danger but also profound psychological stress. Research on disaster psychology indicates that exposure to floods can trigger acute stress reactions, anxiety, and in some cases, post-traumatic stress disorder. Studies conducted after the 2010 Pakistan floods (one of the largest in modern history) showed increased rates of mental health disorders among survivors, including symptoms of hypervigilance, insomnia, and emotional distress.

During the flood event itself, the immediate stress response can be overwhelming. We face the terrifying prospect of losing our homes, livelihoods, and even loved ones. We must make rapid decisions with limited information, often amid darkness, noise, and confusion.

Yet, the ability to maintain composure during these moments is not simply a matter of personality or innate temperament; it can be learned and practiced. Training in stress management and emotional regulation is common among emergency responders and can be adapted for public education.

BREATHING TECHNIQUES TO MANAGE FEAR AND STRESS

Controlled breathing is one of the simplest yet most effective tools for reducing anxiety and preventing panic during a flood. Panic causes shallow and rapid breathing (hyperventilation), which can exacerbate feelings of dizziness, confusion, and shortness of breath. This can further fuel fear and lead to poor decisions.

Several breathing techniques have been validated in clinical and field settings for their calming effects.

DIAPHRAGMATIC BREATHING (ABDOMINAL BREATHING)

This technique focuses on engaging the diaphragm to encourage slow, deep breaths, which activate the parasympathetic nervous system, the body's "rest-and-digest" mode that counters the stress response.

How to Do It: Sit or stand comfortably. Place one hand on your chest and one on your abdomen. Inhale slowly through the nose for a count of four, feeling the abdomen expand while the chest remains relatively still. Hold your breath for a count of two. Exhale slowly through the mouth for a count of six, feeling the abdomen contract. Repeat for several cycles.

Benefits: This method reduces heart rate and blood pressure, lowers cortisol levels, and improves oxygen exchange, all of which help restore calm.

BOX BREATHING (SQUARE BREATHING)

Popularized by Navy SEALs and other high-stress professions, box breathing is a structured technique to maintain focus and control.

How to Do It: Inhale through the nose for a count of four. Hold your breath for four seconds. Exhale through the mouth for four seconds. Hold your breath for four seconds. Repeat.

Benefits: Box breathing can improve concentration and counteract the erratic breathing patterns caused by anxiety.

4-7-8 BREATHING TECHNIQUE

Developed by Dr. Andrew Weil, this technique is designed to quickly reduce anxiety and induce relaxation.

How to Do It: Inhale quietly through the nose for four seconds. Hold the breath for seven seconds. Exhale forcefully through the mouth for eight seconds. Repeat three to four times.

Benefits: This breathing pattern slows the heartbeat and calms the nervous system, which can be particularly useful when facing overwhelming flood conditions.

MENTAL STRATEGIES TO MANAGE FEAR AND STRESS

Beyond breathing exercises, mental strategies can greatly enhance resilience during floods. Combining a mindset of preparedness and acceptance with practical cognitive tools can empower you to make sound decisions under pressure.

MENTAL REHEARSAL AND VISUALIZATION

Studies in sports psychology and military training show that mentally rehearsing scenarios improves performance during actual events. In flood preparedness, visualizing safe actions, such as locating evacuation routes, securing family members, or using flotation devices, can reduce the shock of the moment.

Application: Before a flood occurs, envision your flood response plans. During the event, consciously recalling these rehearsals can foster a sense of control.

GROUNDING TECHNIQUES

When fear threatens to overwhelm, grounding strategies help anchor awareness in the present moment, preventing runaway panic.

Example: Use the "5-4-3-2-1" technique to identify five things you can see, four you can touch, three you can hear, two you can smell, and one you can taste. This sensory focus interrupts spiraling anxiety and redirects attention to tangible reality.

COGNITIVE RESTRUCTURING

This technique involves challenging catastrophic or irrational thoughts and replacing them with realistic assessments.

Example: Instead of thinking "I'm going to drown," reframe the thought to "I have a life jacket and a plan to reach high ground." This reframing can reduce hopelessness and increase problem-solving capacity.

BREAKING DOWN THE SITUATION

Flooding can feel overwhelming when viewed as a single massive problem. Breaking it down into smaller, manageable tasks, such as "secure the children," "gather important documents," or "move to the second floor," can prevent paralysis by analysis and focus energy on achievable goals.

MAINTAINING SOCIAL CONNECTIONS

Communication with family members or emergency responders can mitigate feelings of isolation and fear. Even when separated, verbalizing actions ("I'm moving to the upstairs bedroom now") when you are within earshot can reassure others and reduce panic.

Public awareness campaigns emphasized the importance of avoiding unnecessary travel and staying indoors when floodwaters rose. After Hurricane Sandy, community centers served as hubs for disseminating information and providing psychological support. Many survivors reported using breathing and grounding techniques taught in prior preparedness workshops, which helped them maintain clear thinking while relocating valuables and waiting for rescue.

PRACTICAL ADVICE FOR STAYING CALM DURING A FLOOD

Prepare a Flood Survival Kit: This suggestion bears repeating. Having a ready kit reduces anxiety by ensuring access to essentials: water, food, medications, flashlights, batteries, and communication devices.

Stay Informed Through Trusted Sources: Tune into official updates via radio, smartphone alerts, or emergency broadcasts. Accurate information counteracts rumors and uncertainty.

Avoid Risky Behaviors: Do not attempt to drive or walk through floodwaters. Just six inches of moving water can knock an adult off their feet; one foot of water can sweep away a vehicle.

Use Personal Affirmations: Repeating calming phrases like "I am safe, I am prepared" can help anchor the mind during distress.

Keep Children and Vulnerable Individuals Reassured: Children are particularly sensitive to parental cues. Maintaining a composed demeanor can help alleviate their fears.

THE ROLE OF EMERGENCY SERVICES AND COMMUNITY SUPPORT

Emergency responders receive training not only in technical rescue but also in psychological first aid. Survivors should be aware that seeking help, whether from neighbors, shelters, or first responders, is a sign of strength, not weakness.

Many disaster relief organizations now incorporate mental health support alongside physical aid during and after floods, recognizing the interplay between mental calmness and survival.

COMMUNICATION

In a flood emergency, communication is a lifeline. The ability to exchange timely, accurate information, from coordinating with family members to receiving official evacuation orders, is essential for survival, situational awareness, and support coordination.

One of the greatest risks during a flood is being isolated. Floodwaters frequently sever roads and bridges, trap people in their homes, or make travel impossible. In these conditions, having a solid communication plan with family, neighbors, and local authorities can save lives.

FAMILY COMMUNICATION PLANS

The time to prepare for communication challenges is before the flood begins. Every household should have a preestablished emergency communication plan that includes:

Primary and Alternate Contacts: Assign an out-of-area contact person for the family. In disaster zones, local lines are often jammed, but long-distance lines may still function. Each family member should know this person's phone number and how to check in with them.

Meeting Points: Designate a primary meeting location outside the immediate flood zone and an alternative in case the first becomes inaccessible.

Roles and Responsibilities: Determine who is responsible for contacting whom, who gathers emergency supplies, and who helps vulnerable members like children or the elderly.

During an active flood, it's not uncommon for family members to become separated or stranded, which can quickly lead to confusion and panic. To maintain communication when voice calls fail, it's helpful to use group messaging apps such as WhatsApp or Signal, which often work better on weak networks. Messages should be brief but informative, including your current location, safety status, and intended next steps. This ensures everyone stays informed without overwhelming limited bandwidth or battery life.

If separation does occur, it's generally safer to avoid attempting to locate others by traveling through flooded areas. Instead, coordinate a reunification plan using predesignated meeting points or official shelters. Moving through floodwaters unnecessarily increases risk and can delay emergency response efforts. Having a clear, calm communication plan in place helps keep everyone focused and improves the likelihood of a safe outcome.

COMMUNITY AND NEIGHBOR NETWORKS

Community ties can be vital during a flood. In many disasters, neighbors are the first responders before official help arrives. Neighborhood watch groups, homeowners associations, and local preparedness initiatives should develop flood-specific communication strategies, including:

- Shared contact lists for elderly or disabled residents who may need assistance.
- Local check-in protocols to ensure everyone is accounted for.
- Group messaging systems (like GroupMe or Slack) to disseminate information quickly.

Local governments can facilitate these networks by encouraging "whole community preparedness," a concept promoted by FEMA that emphasizes inclusive, grassroots communication structures to reach all demographics, especially those who are traditionally underserved or isolated.

COMMUNICATION WITH EMERGENCY SERVICES AND AUTHORITIES

Reliable, two-way communication with local emergency services is critical. This includes:

- Heeding official alerts and advisories from municipal governments, the National Weather Service, and emergency management agencies.
- Reporting emergencies accurately: When calling 911, provide your precise location, the number of people involved, and the nature of the emergency. Be concise and clear because call volume will be high during a flood.
- Listening to guidance: If authorities order an evacuation, comply immediately unless doing so would place you in greater danger.

Many regions offer reverse 911 systems, community alert texts, or integrated public alert and warning systems that can notify residents via cell phones, emails, or sirens. Ensure you're registered for these services ahead of time.

EMERGENCY RADIOS, CELL PHONES, AND APPS

In an era dominated by smartphones and digital connectivity, it's easy to take communication infrastructure for granted. However, floods often disable cell towers, jam networks, or cut power, making alternative technologies essential for staying informed.

The NOAA Weather Radio system is a critical tool in flood situations. Operated by the National Oceanic and Atmospheric Administration, this system provides 24/7 broadcasts of weather and hazard alerts. Key features include:

- Battery-powered or hand-crank options that work during power outages.
- Specific Area Message Encoding that allows users to receive alerts tailored to their county or local area.
- Public alerts that include flood warnings, evacuation notices, and AMBER alerts.

Radios with AM/FM bands can also provide information from local stations, especially when internet service is down. In many cases, local broadcasters will work with emergency management to deliver up-to-the-minute updates on shelters, road closures, and safety tips.

CELL PHONES AND SMARTPHONES

When functional, smartphones are indispensable tools for managing a flood crisis. Here's how to optimize their use:

ENABLE EMERGENCY ALERTS: Most modern phones support wireless emergency alerts, which send government-issued notifications about imminent threats.

INSTALL RELEVANT APPS: I find these apps useful.

- **FEMA App:** Provides real-time alerts, disaster resources, and shelter locations.
- **Red Cross Emergency App:** Offers step-by-step guidance during various emergencies, including floods.
- **Zello:** Turns your phone into a walkie-talkie, which can be useful if cellular voice service is down.
- **Life360:** Tracks family members and allows group check-ins.

CONSERVE BATTERY LIFE: Reduce screen brightness, close unused apps, turn off background data usage, and use battery-saver mode.

USE MESSAGING OVER VOICE: SMS texts are more likely to go through than voice calls in congested networks.

SOCIAL MEDIA AND CROWDSOURCED INFORMATION

Social media platforms like Twitter, Facebook, and Nextdoor can be useful for obtaining real-time updates, such as flood extent, road closures, and safe routes, but they should be used cautiously. During emergencies, misinformation spreads rapidly. Always cross-reference posts with official sources, such as:

- National Weather Service (@NWS)
- Local emergency management departments
- Verified government or relief organization pages

Use hashtags relevant to your area (e.g., #HoustonFlood or #CAStorm) to track localized reports. Facebook's Safety Check feature allows users to mark themselves as safe during disasters, helping reduce panic among extended friends and family.

WHAT TO DO IF COMMUNICATION LINES ARE DOWN

When flood conditions disrupt or destroy communication infrastructure, staying connected becomes extremely difficult, but not impossible. This was evident during Hurricane Maria in 2017, when nearly all of Puerto Rico lost cell and internet service for weeks. In such situations, having preestablished backup methods and contingency plans can be lifesaving.

When using limited tools such as short-range radios or brief windows of power availability, a fixed communication schedule helps conserve resources and manage expectations. For example, tuning in to emergency broadcasts like NOAA radio at the top of each hour ensures you catch important updates without draining batteries. Similarly, setting designated times, such as 9 a.m. and 5 p.m., for attempting to check in with family or emergency contacts provides structure and reassurance. Even if a message doesn't go through every time, everyone involved will know when to expect an update and when to try again.

During the 2022 floods in Pakistan, many survivors were located by rescuers because they prearranged check-in times with family. When the check-in failed, that absence alone served as a red flag.

USE TWO-WAY RADIOS OR WALKIE-TALKIES

Short-range two-way radios like general mobile radio service (GMRS) radios and family radio service (FRS) radios are both useful tools for communication within a neighborhood, building, or small area during a flood, especially when cell networks are down. They do not rely on cell towers or Wi-Fi and are especially valuable in rural or mountainous regions. GMRS radios offer greater range, up to several miles in open conditions, and typically provide clearer, more reliable signals. However, they require a license to operate legally in the US, which involves a small fee and an application through the FCC.

On the other hand, FRS radios are license-free and user-friendly, making them a convenient option for most families. While their range is more limited (typically under a mile in urban or obstructed environments), they are still effective for neighborhood or household communication during an emergency. Both types can be critical lifelines during floods, particularly when combined with a family communication plan and regular practice.

SIGNAL FOR HELP WITHOUT ELECTRONICS

If completely cut off, traditional signaling techniques remain effective:

VISUAL SIGNALS: Place large white cloths, bright colors, or reflective materials on rooftops or out of windows to signal distress.

SOUND SIGNALS: Three short whistle blasts, repeated periodically, is an internationally recognized distress call.

WRITTEN MESSAGES: Use waterproof markers to write messages on visible surfaces for rescuers (e.g., "3 PEOPLE INSIDE—NEED MEDICAL HELP").

See How to Signal for Help If You're Trapped or in Danger on page 148 for more on this topic.

INTEGRATING COMMUNICATION INTO YOUR PREPAREDNESS PLAN

In a flood, having the tools and knowledge to stay informed and connected can prevent panic, guide your next steps, and ultimately save lives. The most effective communication during a flood doesn't happen spontaneously, it results from foresight and organization.

Here are key elements to integrate into your broader flood preparedness strategy:

- **Backup Power:** Stockpile power banks, solar chargers, and extra batteries.
- **Multiple Communication Tools:** Don't rely solely on one method. Combine phones, radios, apps, and analog signaling.
- **Redundant Contact Plans:** Create laminated contact cards for family members that include phone numbers, email addresses, emergency contacts, and key apps.
- **Regular Drills:** Practice emergency communication as part of flood evacuation or shelter-in-place drills. Include children and vulnerable individuals.

HANDLING VARIOUS FLOOD SCENARIOS: EVACUATING SAFELY

Floods can unfold in a range of ways, some slowly over days, others explosively within minutes. One of the most critical decisions you may face during a flood is whether to evacuate or shelter in place. Failing to evacuate when needed can result in entrapment, while evacuating too late can place you in even greater danger. Understanding when to leave, how to do so safely, and what to bring can spell the difference between a harrowing ordeal and a well-managed emergency.

WHEN TO EVACUATE: RECOGNIZING THE SIGNS THAT IT'S TIME TO LEAVE

Timing is everything. Waiting just 30 minutes longer can mean missing a narrow window of manageable conditions and getting trapped in rapidly rising floodwaters. Unfortunately, many wait too long, either because they underestimate the risk, hope conditions will improve, or receive conflicting information.

OFFICIAL EVACUATION ORDERS

Always heed official evacuation notices. These may come in the form of:

- Mandatory evacuations issued by local or state authorities, requiring all residents to leave a designated area. These are typically issued when there is a high likelihood of life-threatening conditions.
- Voluntary evacuations, which allow residents to stay but strongly advise departure, particularly for those in vulnerable housing, with medical conditions, or without transportation.

Even without a mandatory evacuation order, there are circumstances under which choosing to leave early can protect your life and reduce hardship. If you live in a low-lying area near rivers, creeks, or within designated flood zones, the risk of sudden inundation is significantly higher. These areas are often the first to flood and can become dangerous very quickly, especially during heavy rainfall or upstream water releases.

Homes that have flooded before or appear on FEMA floodplain maps are statistically more likely to flood again. Past flooding is a strong indicator of future vulnerability, and staying in place during similar conditions may expose you to repeat losses or life-threatening conditions.

You should also consider evacuating if your region is prone to flash floods. These fast-moving events can be triggered with little warning (sometimes in under an hour), especially in hilly or urban areas with poor drainage. If there's a history of flash flooding near your home or you've seen roadways and creeks quickly overrun during storms, it's safer to get out early rather than risk becoming trapped.

In 2005, many residents of New Orleans chose not to evacuate ahead of Hurricane Katrina. Tragically, the failure to heed evacuation orders led to more than 1,800 deaths, many of which were preventable. Similarly, in the 2018 Kerala floods in India, delayed evacuation contributed to high casualties despite days of rain warnings.

ENVIRONMENTAL CUES AND SITUATIONAL AWARENESS

Official warnings are essential, but during a flood, your personal observations may offer the earliest and most accurate indicators of danger. Paying close attention to environmental cues can help you make timely decisions, even before authorities issue alerts. Rapidly rising water levels, particularly when heavy rain continues to fall or the ground is already saturated, often signal that flooding is about to worsen. If water has started entering your home, pooling in the yard, or creeping up driveways and streets, it's a strong indication that conditions are escalating quickly.

Other warning signs include washed-out roads, mudslides, or increasing speed and volume in local streams or drainage systems. These suggest that nearby water systems are overwhelmed and pose serious risks. A sudden loss of power or communication, especially if paired with worsening weather, can mean infrastructure is failing and help may not be immediately available. In these situations, waiting for official direction may be too late. Trust your senses, and if the environment around you feels increasingly unsafe, it's wise to act immediately and seek higher ground or evacuate.

If you feel unsafe or are unsure about your ability to remain secure in your location, it is always safer to leave earlier rather than later. Authorities often struggle to assist during peak danger, and you should not assume help will arrive in time.

HOW TO SAFELY EVACUATE ON FOOT OR BY VEHICLE

Whether you evacuate by car, on foot, or by bicycle, carefully consider your route and timing. Floodwaters are deceptive; what appears shallow and harmless may in fact be deadly.

- Never attempt to drive or walk through moving water. Again, just six inches of water can knock over an adult, and 12 to 24 inches can float a vehicle. According to the National Weather Service, more than half of flood-related drownings occur when vehicles are driven into hazardous floodwater.
- Stick to high ground and known routes. Avoid shortcuts through poorly lit or low-lying areas.
- Use designated evacuation routes. These are identified by local emergency services and chosen for their elevation, accessibility, and likelihood of being cleared and monitored.

EVACUATING BY VEHICLE

Evacuating by vehicle is often the fastest and most efficient way to reach safety during a flood, but it also carries specific dangers. Roads may be washed out, bridges compromised, and underpasses completely submerged. It's essential to plan your route in advance and not rely solely on GPS, as these systems may not reflect real-time closures. Printed maps with multiple exit routes can be lifesaving if technology fails or detours become necessary. Fuel up as early as possible because gas stations frequently run dry or shut down once an evacuation order is in place. Keep a stocked emergency kit in your car, including water, blankets, jumper cables, a first aid kit, and nonperishable snacks.

When driving, avoid areas prone to flooding, such as low-lying roads, underpasses, and bridges that may be structurally unsound. Drive slowly and steadily, even in heavy traffic. Speeding or tailgating increases the risk of hydroplaning or losing control.

During the 2015 South Carolina floods, hundreds of people required rescue after attempting to drive through submerged roads, often ignoring posted warnings. Conversely, in Houston during Hurricane Harvey, coordinated efforts like traffic rerouting and timely highway closures helped prevent many vehicular drownings, even amid unprecedented rainfall. Staying alert and cautious behind the wheel can make all the difference.

EVACUATING ON FOOT

Evacuating on foot may become necessary when driving is impossible due to high water, blocked roads, or lack of access to transportation. While walking can offer more flexibility in navigating difficult terrain, it comes with serious risks that require careful preparation. Wear layered, weather-appropriate clothing, waterproof boots, and a jacket to protect against the elements. Visibility is crucial, especially in low light. Use a flashlight or wear a bright vest to ensure you're seen by others, including rescuers. A walking stick or pole can help test water depth and check for unstable ground or submerged hazards.

Whenever possible, avoid walking through floodwater. It can be contaminated with sewage, chemicals, or debris, and may conceal sharp objects or sudden drop-offs. Dangerous currents can form even in water just a foot deep. Stick to sidewalks or higher ground, and if you're in a group, stay close together and move slowly to maintain safety and communication. Pack only essential items in a waterproof bag or backpack, keeping your hands free for balance. If you must cross standing water, aim for the shallowest point and move diagonally with the current to reduce resistance and maintain stability.

WHAT TO TAKE WITH YOU IF YOU MUST LEAVE QUICKLY

Flood evacuations often happen with little or no warning. To prepare for a sudden departure, assemble a go-bag or emergency evacuation kit in advance and store it in a location that is easy to access, ideally on an upper level of your home.

ESSENTIALS FOR A FLOOD EVACUATION KIT

IDENTIFICATION AND CRITICAL DOCUMENTS

❍ Driver's licenses, passports, insurance policies, home deed/lease

❍ Birth certificates, medical records

❍ Waterproof bag or folder for storage

COMMUNICATION AND NAVIGATION

❍ Fully charged cell phone and power banks

❍ Emergency contact list (paper copy)

❍ Printed maps with marked evacuation routes

HEALTH AND HYGIENE

❍ First-aid kit

❍ Prescription medications and copies of prescriptions

❍ Face masks, hand sanitizer, feminine hygiene products, toothbrush, etc.

BASIC NECESSITIES

❍ Flashlight with extra batteries

❍ Multi-tool or pocketknife

❍ Cash in small denominations (ATMs may be down)

❍ Emergency whistle

FOOD AND WATER

❍ At least one gallon of water per person per day (for three days, if possible)

❍ High-calorie, nonperishable food like energy bars or canned goods

❍ Manual can opener

CLOTHING AND SHELTER

❍ Extra socks and undergarments

❍ Emergency blankets or sleeping bags

❍ Ponchos or tarps

FOR CHILDREN AND VULNERABLE INDIVIDUALS

❍ Diapers, formula, small toys, or comfort items

❍ Mobility aids, hearing aids, spare eyeglasses

FOR PETS

❍ Pet food, leash, collapsible bowls (for water or food), travel crate

VACCINATION RECORDS AND MEDICATIONS

❍ Having a smaller version of your emergency kit in your car is also advisable in case you're caught away from home when evacuation is necessary.

HANDLING VARIOUS FLOOD SCENARIOS: SHELTERING IN PLACE

In some flood situations, evacuation may be impossible or inadvisable. Roads may be impassable, the threat may emerge too quickly to escape, or you may be sheltering vulnerable individuals for whom travel is too dangerous. In these cases, the only safe option is to remain inside and shelter in place. Far from being a passive decision, successful sheltering demands deliberate action, forethought, and real-time problem-solving.

HOW TO STAY SAFE IF YOU'RE UNABLE TO EVACUATE

Elevate above the water. This is the fundamental rule of sheltering during a flood. Water levels can rise with terrifying speed, especially in flash floods or with dam/levee failures, so your safest location is often a higher floor, attic, or structurally sound roof.

- **Identify Your Safest Shelter Area in Advance:** Ideally, this is an upper-level interior room with few windows, structurally sound flooring, and easy access to escape routes such as stairs or an exterior window.
- **Avoid Basements and Ground-Level Rooms:** These areas are the first to flood and can trap you if the water rises quickly. Tragically, many victims of floods like the 2004 Boscastle flood in the UK and those caused by Hurricane Harvey died because they remained in or returned to basements after water receded temporarily.

- **Plan an Escape Route to the Roof:** Keep a ladder accessible if no indoor stairs lead there. However, only go to the roof if you are certain the structure will hold and you are attempting to signal for rescue.

In 2011, during the Thailand floods, hundreds of thousands sheltered for weeks in upper levels of homes and businesses. Their survival was largely due to advanced preparation in the form of elevated safe zones, stored supplies, and communication with authorities.

SEALING AND FORTIFYING THE HOME

Even if water is already entering your home, you can take measures to reduce further intrusion and slow its spread.

- **Seal Doors with Plastic Sheeting and Duct Tape:** Create makeshift water barriers by taping heavy-duty plastic sheets across door seams, vents, or window frames.
- **Place Sandbags or Water Barriers at Entrances:** Even a few strategically placed bags can delay water intrusion long enough to escape or preserve interior spaces.
- **Unplug and Elevate Electrical Appliances:** If you have time, shut off power at the circuit breaker (especially if flooding has reached outlets). Never stand in water while doing this.
- **Use Furniture and Plastic Bins to Create Raised Surfaces on Which to Store Items:** Stack items like food, documents, and electronics on tables or beds (ideally sealed in plastic containers or garbage bags).

These steps do not make a house floodproof, but they buy time to move valuables, stay safe, or wait for rescue.

COMMUNICATING YOUR LOCATION TO AUTHORITIES AND LOVED ONES

Ensuring that emergency responders and loved ones know your location and condition helps prioritize rescue efforts and alleviates uncertainty for those trying to reach you.

If you're trapped or unable to evacuate safely, your first step should be to contact emergency services. Call 911 (or your country's equivalent), and clearly state your name, address, and current situation. Be concise, as phone lines are often overloaded during disasters. If your area supports it, texting 911 may be more effective as texts can sometimes get through when voice calls cannot.

In the absence of cellular service, other methods can bridge the communication gap. Use emergency or disaster apps from government agencies, many of which offer built-in check-in tools. If those aren't working, platforms like Facebook's Safety Check may allow you to mark yourself safe. When signals return briefly, send short prewritten status messages to designated contacts. Even limited communication can reassure family and provide crucial updates.

In total communication blackouts, visual cues become essential. As previously mentioned, hanging a bright cloth from a window or rooftop is a universal distress signal. At night, flashing a flashlight at regular intervals or using a mirror to reflect sunlight during the day can help attract the attention of rescuers in helicopters or boats. These simple actions can help you avoid being overlooked and get you found.

KEEP RECORDS OF COMMUNICATIONS

Keeping notes during a flood is crucial for relief efforts, insurance, and understanding the event. Record who you contacted and when, save messages exchanged, track home conditions and changes in water levels, and monitor your health. This helps support recovery and provides important evidence if needed later.

ADDITIONAL TIPS FOR SUCCESSFUL SHELTER-IN-PLACE SITUATIONS

- **Conserve Resources:** Ration water and food based on estimated time of isolation.

- **Limit Movement:** Avoid unnecessary risk. Wet stairs, floating debris, and structural weakness can cause injury.
- **Stay Alert for New Dangers:** Listen for structural creaks, gas smells, water shifts, or signs of mold or contamination.
- **Manage Waste and Sanitation:** If toilets are unusable, create a temporary bucket toilet with disinfectants like bleach or lime. Use plastic bags with sealable containers for human waste. These bags would go in the buckets.

EMOTIONAL WELL-BEING WHILE SHELTERING IN PLACE

Being isolated during a flood is psychologically demanding. Stress, fear, and the unknown can compound to create panic or depression. To preserve morale:

- **Stay Busy:** Assign small tasks to each person: checking water levels, recording observations, maintaining supplies.
- **Talk and Listen:** If you are with others, keep conversation going. If alone, write down your thoughts and plans.
- **Practice Calming Techniques:** Deep breathing, meditation, and visualization exercises help control anxiety and prevent rash decisions.
- **Limit Exposure to Alarming Media:** While it's important to stay informed, avoid compulsively consuming distressing updates.

AFTER THE FLOOD: WHEN TO EXIT YOUR SHELTER

Even after floodwaters begin to recede, significant dangers often remain. It is crucial not to leave your shelter until authorities have declared the area safe and the water has fully drained from all access routes. Before exiting, carefully assess your surroundings for any structural damage to buildings or roads, and ensure you have appropriate footwear and clothing to protect yourself from contaminated debris.

Exercise extreme caution, as hazards like electrocution from downed power lines, unstable structures, gas leaks, and polluted floodwaters can pose serious risks long after the storm has passed.

HANDLING VARIOUS FLOOD SCENARIOS: DEALING WITH POWER OUTAGES

Power outages are one of the most common and dangerous consequences of flooding. Whether caused by submerged electrical infrastructure, downed lines, or proactive shutdowns by utility companies to prevent electrocution, power loss can dramatically compound the challenges of surviving a flood. A loss of electricity affects lighting, heating, communication, water pumps, refrigeration, and critical medical devices, sometimes all at once.

STAYING WARM AND DRY

If your home loses heat and electricity during a flood, particularly in cooler climates or seasons, the risk of hypothermia increases dramatically. Even moderate indoor temperatures can feel dangerously cold if you're wet, stationary, or undernourished.

Key strategies to retain body heat:

- **Layer Clothing:** Wear multiple thin layers rather than one thick one. Wool and synthetic materials retain heat better than cotton when wet.
- **Insulate your environment:** Block drafts using towels, plastic sheeting, or even duct-taped garbage bags. Hang blankets over windows and doorways to trap warmth in a single room.
- **Designate a "warm zone":** Choose one interior room to consolidate people, body heat, candles, and other safe heat sources. Avoid large, open spaces that are harder to keep warm.
- **Share body heat:** If appropriate, huddle together under blankets. This is especially effective with infants, who are more susceptible to cold.

If you must use alternate heat sources, such as propane heaters or fireplaces, ensure they are rated for indoor use and properly ventilated. Fires and carbon monoxide poisoning are common causes of death during winter storms and floods, many of which occur after the initial disaster phase.

In the aftermath of the 2021 Texas freeze and flooding, dozens of people died not from weather exposure but from unsafe attempts to generate heat indoors, such as running grills, stoves, or cars in enclosed garages. Proper precautions are nonnegotiable.

PRESERVING FOOD AND WATER

A prolonged power outage poses a serious threat to food safety, as refrigerated and frozen items can spoil rapidly, increasing the risk of foodborne illness, particularly when medical services may be overwhelmed or hard to reach.

To reduce this risk, keep refrigerator and freezer doors closed as much as possible. A full refrigerator can keep food cold for about four hours without power, while a full freezer can maintain safe temperatures for 24 to 48 hours. Avoid opening the doors unnecessarily to preserve the cold air. Using a refrigerator/freezer thermometer helps you accurately determine if food is still safe, eliminating guesswork. Prioritize consuming perishable foods first (fresh fruits, vegetables, dairy, and leftovers) before moving on to canned or packaged goods. Any food that has been above 40°F (4°C) for more than two hours, especially meat, dairy, and items labeled "keep refrigerated," should be discarded to avoid illness.

If water systems are compromised, boil water before drinking. If boiling isn't possible, treat water with purification tablets or household bleach, using eight drops per gallon of clear water, stirring well, and letting it sit for 30 minutes. Remember that floodwaters can contaminate tap water even when municipal services appear functional. Stay informed by monitoring updates from local public health authorities or using a battery-powered NOAA radio.

PREVENTING CARBON MONOXIDE POISONING

Carbon monoxide (CO) is a colorless, odorless gas that can become deadly within minutes when inhaled in enclosed or poorly ventilated spaces. It is produced by common household and emergency equipment, including generators, gas stoves or ovens, portable propane heaters, charcoal grills, and car engines left running. Because it cannot be detected by human senses, proper precautions and detectors are essential to prevent CO poisoning, especially during power outages or flood emergencies when alternative heating and cooking methods are often used indoors.

Post-Hurricane Laura in 2020, carbon monoxide poisoning caused more deaths in Louisiana than the storm itself. Most incidents stemmed from improper generator placement. Education and vigilance are essential.

Best practices to prevent CO poisoning:

- **Never Use Gas-Powered Equipment Indoors:** This includes garages, basements, or enclosed porches, even if windows are open.
- **Operate Generators Outdoors:** The generators should be at least 20 feet from any window, door, or vent. Ensure exhaust is directed away from living spaces.
- **Install Battery-Powered Carbon Monoxide Detectors:** These are inexpensive and potentially lifesaving.
- **Be Alert for Symptoms:** Headache, dizziness, nausea, confusion, or fainting may indicate CO exposure. Evacuate immediately and seek fresh air and medical attention.

USING BACKUP POWER SOURCES SAFELY

Using backup power sources safely is crucial during floods and power outages to maintain essential functions like lighting, communication, and medical equipment operation. However, improper use can lead to serious hazards, including fires and electrocution.

Generators are a common choice for backup power but must be handled with care. Always operate generators outdoors on dry, level ground, ideally under a canopy for weather protection but never inside or in enclosed spaces. Position the generator at least 20 feet away from doors and windows to prevent carbon monoxide buildup inside the home. Appliances should be plugged directly into the generator using heavy-duty, grounded extension cords. Never connect a generator to a home's electrical system by plugging it into a wall outlet, a dangerous practice known as back feeding.

Pay close attention to the generator's wattage rating to avoid overloading, which can cause equipment damage or fire. Store gasoline safely in approved containers kept in secure, well-ventilated areas away from living spaces. When you're done using a generator, always allow it to cool completely before refueling, since spilling fuel on the engine parts while they're still hot can ignite instantly. Using fuel stabilizers is recommended for long-term gasoline storage to maintain engine performance and prevent damage.

In flood-prone areas, consider placing the generator on a raised platform or wheeled cart to keep it above potential floodwaters while maintaining proper ventilation. This helps protect your backup power source from water damage and ensures safe operation during emergencies.

Battery packs and **solar chargers** offer safer and more convenient alternatives to fuel-powered generators for keeping essential electronics and medical devices running during power outages. Portable battery banks are great for charging phones, radios, flashlights, and small fans. Be sure to keep them fully charged before storms and perform regular maintenance to ensure reliability.

Solar chargers have become increasingly efficient and are especially useful for extended emergencies. When selecting one, look for rugged, waterproof designs with multiple USB ports and built-in storage to maximize their usefulness.

For more power, lithium-based portable power stations can run small appliances and last for several days if managed properly. Models equipped with AC outlets and pure sine wave inverters are particularly valuable for sensitive equipment like CPAP machines.

These battery-powered solutions are especially important in settings where fuel generators are impractical or not allowed, such as in apartments, senior living facilities, or designated flood shelters. They provide a quieter, cleaner, and often more portable way to maintain essential power during emergencies.

PLANNING FOR MEDICAL NEEDS DURING POWER OUTAGES

For those who depend on electrically powered medical equipment, such as oxygen concentrators, refrigerated insulin, or nebulizers, a power outage can escalate into a life-threatening emergency. Preparing in advance is essential to ensure continuity of care when the grid goes down.

Start by registering with your local utility company and emergency services. Many jurisdictions maintain lists of medically vulnerable residents, giving them priority for power restoration or evacuation during disasters. This simple step can significantly improve your chances of receiving timely support.

Develop a backup power plan tailored to your specific needs. This might include battery packs designed for medical equipment, or identifying the nearest shelter or hospital that has reliable backup power. Keep in mind that medical-grade battery systems should be fully charged and tested regularly to ensure they're ready when needed.

For medications like insulin that require refrigeration, have a dedicated cooler and reusable ice packs ready. Store these medications in watertight containers to protect them from moisture, and ensure you can keep them cool for at least 24 to 48 hours during an outage. Having a self-sufficient plan can be critical, especially since hospitals themselves may experience power strain or flooding and cannot always serve as a guaranteed fallback.

PRACTICAL STEPS TO PREPARE FOR POWER LOSS IN ADVANCE

Before a flood, test flashlights, radios, and spare batteries to ensure everything works as expected. Fully charge all essential devices, including cell phones, power banks, and medical equipment. Fill bathtubs, sinks, or containers with clean water for hygiene use, and freeze bottles of water to help maintain freezer temperatures if the power goes out. Store important documents, medications, and backup supplies in waterproof containers. It's also crucial to review how to safely shut off your home's gas, water, and electrical systems to prevent additional hazards.

During the flood, use lighting carefully and opt for battery-powered options over candles to reduce the risk of fire, especially in homes with children or pets. Monitor battery levels of phones, radios, and other devices, and conserve power when possible. Move electronics and charging equipment to elevated surfaces to avoid water damage. If it's safe, maintain contact with neighbors, particularly those who may need assistance due to medical conditions, age, or limited mobility. These simple but thoughtful actions can help you manage the blackout with greater control and security. Prolonged darkness and isolation can produce disorientation, anxiety, and depression, especially in children or individuals with trauma history. The following activities can help reduce the mental and emotional impacts of extended outages:

- Create a predictable schedule: meal times, updates, check-ins, rest.
- Use games, reading, or storytelling to maintain morale.
- Rotate responsibilities among household members to sustain engagement.
- Use light sources like LED lanterns to simulate daylight.
- Stay focused on controllable actions (managing supplies, checking weather).

Even basic mental stimulation can reduce panic and help household members endure the long hours of uncertainty that come with floods and blackouts.

WHAT TO DO IF CAUGHT IN MOVING WATER

If you are ever caught in moving water, whether by misjudging a crossing, being overtaken by a flash flood, or swept away during evacuation, the difference between survival and tragedy often comes down to a few critical decisions made in moments of extreme stress.

Water is deceptively powerful. It doesn't take a raging torrent or deep river to pose a threat.

The dynamic force of moving water increases exponentially with speed and volume. In flood conditions, especially those caused by heavy rains or dam failures, currents can move faster than anticipated, filled with debris, mud, and unseen hazards beneath the surface.

The Centers for Disease Control and Prevention (CDC) reports that over half of flood-related drownings occur when individuals attempt to drive through floodwaters. Many of these deaths are not from deep waters, but from strong currents that compromise the vehicle's traction and cause it to roll or become submerged.

WHY YOU SHOULD NEVER ENTER FLOODWATERS

Even seemingly shallow or calm floodwaters can conceal multiple hazards, such as:

- **Debris:** Sharp objects, glass, metal, or wood fragments can injure or trap victims.
- **Contaminants:** Sewage, chemicals, fuel, and bacteria can increase the risk of infection or illness.
- **Unstable Ground:** Erosion, sinkholes, or displaced manhole covers can create unexpected drop-offs.
- **Electrocution:** Downed power lines or submerged electrical systems can electrify water without visible signs.
- **Unpredictable Currents:** Fast-moving water may behave erratically, especially around urban structures or natural obstructions.

FLOATING AND AVOIDING SUBMERSION

If you find yourself caught in moving water, the most important rule is to remain calm. Panic can lead to disorientation, exhaustion, and poor decisions. Your immediate goal should be to keep your airway above water while conserving energy.

To do this, float on your back with your feet pointed downstream. This position allows you to see where you're going and helps avoid collisions with debris or obstacles. Keep your head above water and your arms slightly extended for balance. It's crucial to keep your feet up rather than trying to stand or walk in strong currents, as your feet could become trapped in debris, increasing the risk of entrapment and submersion.

If you must swim, use a defensive posture by floating on your back with a gentle flutter kick and sculling motion of your hands. This approach conserves energy and maintains visibility while helping you steer. Avoid fighting the current, as this is often exhausting and ineffective. Instead, focus on controlling your direction and looking for safer spots where the water slows or widens. This "float-and-steer" method is widely taught by rescue organizations such as the American Red Cross and swift water rescue technicians (a specialized rescuer that saves people in fast-moving water) as the safest way to navigate moving water.

WHAT TO DO IF SWEPT AWAY

Being swept away by floodwaters is terrifying but not always fatal. Survivors often credit basic survival techniques, whether learned beforehand or improvised, as crucial to staying alive. The first priority is to stay calm and breathe slowly and purposefully. Panic and hyperventilation can cause drowning even in shallow water. If you take on water, cough it out and focus on controlling your airway above all else.

As you move downstream, look for calmer water where the current slows, such as the inside of river bends, behind obstacles, or in natural depressions. These areas might offer a chance to steer out of the main flow. Swim with the current instead of against it, using its momentum to angle yourself toward safety. This technique, known as "ferrying," is more effective than fighting the water head-on.

If you see large, stable objects like logs or debris piles, try to grab them only if it won't force you underwater. Many objects can roll or shift unexpectedly, so be cautious. Shout for help if others are nearby, as your location may be noted by rescuers. If you get pulled under by a hydraulic (created when water flows over a ledge or rock, then recirculates powerfully upstream) or eddy (a pool of water flowing upstream against the main current), don't fight it. Instead, tuck into a tight ball to stay buoyant and allow the water to release you, as most people resurface after a few seconds when calm and compact.

In the 2015 Texas Memorial Day floods, several survivors were pulled from raging waters after managing to float downstream and grab onto trees or debris until rescuers reached them. Their experiences underscore the importance of knowing how to "go with the flow" while staying oriented and alert.

USING OBJECTS AS FLOTATION DEVICES

Improvising flotation can be a lifesaving tactic during a flood, especially when conditions shift rapidly and there's no time to access proper gear. Everyday household or outdoor items can serve as effective flotation aids if used correctly and with caution.

Plastic bottles and jugs, particularly those that are empty or partially filled, trap air and offer strong buoyancy. Tying them together or securing them under clothing can enhance stability. Airtight coolers and storage bins also float well and can support significant weight if held under the chest or arms. Even a backpack or duffel bag filled with clothes or gear can serve as a makeshift flotation device. Car tires or inner tubes, though bulky, can support a person if found floating nearby; just be mindful of the risk of getting entangled. Foam cushions or outdoor seat pads are also helpful because they're lightweight, water-resistant, and often overlooked.

For best results, keep flotation devices under your chest or armpits to help maintain a horizontal, face-up position in the water. Avoid clinging to items vertically, as this can cause tipping and submersion. If possible, use belts or straps to secure items to your body, keeping your hands free for maneuvering. Always remain alert to debris, branches, and other hazards that could entangle or trap you. Smart, quick use of available objects can greatly increase your chances of staying afloat and being seen by rescuers.

PSYCHOLOGICAL AND PHYSICAL CONSIDERATIONS

Surviving fast-moving water requires physical strength and skills as well as mental resilience and emotional control. Staying calm and focused can conserve precious energy and improve your chances of making it through safely.

Exhaustion sets in quickly, as cold, rushing water can sap your strength in minutes. Instead of fighting the current aggressively, use energy-saving techniques like floating on your back or drifting with the flow until you can reach safety. Disorientation is common, especially in murky water where visibility is low. If you get submerged, look for bubbles or light to help orient yourself toward the surface.

Managing fear is crucial. Panic can cause you to make dangerous mistakes, so use simple mantras like "breathe, float, focus" to steady your mind. While fear is natural, keeping it in check allows clearer thinking and better decision-making. If injured, address wounds or broken limbs only after ensuring you stay afloat, and maintain steady breathing, as survival depends first on staying above water. See Dealing with Fear and Anxiety on page 152 for more on this topic.

SPECIAL CONSIDERATIONS

In any emergency, certain groups face significantly higher risks. During floods where physical displacement, disrupted routines, and environmental dangers converge rapidly, the vulnerability of children, the elderly, and people with disabilities becomes magnified. Ensuring their safety is not simply a matter of compassion, it is a public safety imperative.

SAFETY AND COMFORT FOR CHILDREN

Children are more susceptible to hypothermia, dehydration, injury, and shock. Their smaller size makes them physically less stable in floodwaters; even shallow currents can knock them over. Additionally, they may not fully understand the gravity of the situation or be able to react appropriately in emergencies.

EMOTIONAL REASSURANCE

During stressful events, children look to adults for cues. Calm and clear communication, physical reassurance, and simple explanations are critical. According to the American Academy of Pediatrics, using age-appropriate language to explain what is happening and what steps are being taken for safety can significantly reduce trauma and fear.

ESSENTIALS TO KEEP ON HAND FOR CHILDREN

- ❍ Diapers, wipes, and sanitation supplies
- ❍ Baby formula or breast milk storage containers
- ❍ Child-safe medications
- ❍ Identification and contact cards in their pockets or on lanyards
- ❍ Comfort items (stuffed toys, blankets)
- ❍ Noise-canceling headphones or quiet games to reduce sensory overload

SAFETY ACTIONS

Always keep small children close by during evacuations to ensure their safety, either carrying them or holding their hand firmly. Dress them in bright or reflective clothing to increase visibility, and label their clothes with contact information in case of separation. Never leave children unattended during a flood, even in places that might seem safe, like upper floors or inside vehicles.

During Hurricane Katrina, many children were separated from families during chaotic evacuations. The use of laminated ID cards and wristbands with contact info helped reunite dozens of children with parents in the aftermath. Preparing these in advance can prevent heartbreak in emergencies.

ELDERLY INDIVIDUALS: MOBILITY AND HEALTH ISSUES

Older adults may have difficulty walking long distances, climbing stairs, or carrying emergency supplies. Vision and hearing impairments further compound their challenges. Elderly individuals living alone are less likely to receive timely information or assistance during an evacuation. Community and family communication plans must explicitly account for them.

Medication and medical equipment are critical components of preparedness for those with chronic illnesses such as diabetes or heart disease. Preparing for seniors involves assembling a clearly labeled emergency go-bag containing a full list of medications, medical documents, glasses, hearing aids, extra batteries, and mobility aids like canes or walkers. Whenever possible, duplicate medications should be stored in waterproof containers to prevent damage. Including a whistle or other signaling device can help alert rescuers if the individual becomes trapped. It's also important to keep an emergency contact list both taped to the inside of their door and stored in their wallet or purse for quick access.

Safety strategies include coordinating with neighbors or building managers to ensure regular check-ins, enrolling seniors in community registries maintained by local emergency services, and practicing evacuation drills to familiarize them with stairways, exits, and vehicle access. Since many older adults may feel distressed when removed from familiar surroundings, adding comfort items such as a small photo album, a favorite radio, or familiar scents like hand lotion can provide important emotional grounding during emergencies.

In Japan's 2011 tsunami disaster, nearly 56 percent of those who died were over 65 years old. Studies cited poor mobility, social isolation, and uncoordinated evacuation strategies as primary contributors. This underscores the need to tailor emergency responses for older populations with targeted planning.

PEOPLE WITH DISABILITIES

During floods, those with disabilities encounter a wide range of challenges shaped by the nature of their physical, sensory, cognitive, or psychological conditions. Effective emergency preparedness requires proactive inclusion of their needs.

Personal evacuation plans should be tailored for each individual and reviewed annually. Identifying support networks such as neighbors, caregivers, and friends beforehand ensures timely assistance during emergencies. Emergency kits must be customized to include disability-specific items like assistive devices, extra batteries, specialized dietary supplies, and communication aids.

MOBILITY DISABILITIES

Keep wheelchairs, walkers, or scooters elevated when not in use to prevent water damage. Protect these vehicles with waterproof covers and clear labels. Those using a power wheelchair should have a manual backup available. Portable ramps can help navigate inaccessible routes, and practicing evacuation routes ahead of time allows assessment of accessibility challenges.

Those with mobility challenges should register with local emergency services for priority evacuation and coordinate with neighbors or disability organizations to establish a support network.

HEARING AND VISION IMPAIRMENTS

Access to text-based alert systems and vibrating alarms is crucial. Label important items in braille or large print, and provide whistles or bells that can alert others in case of emergency.

COGNITIVE DISABILITY OR NEURODIVERGENCE

Maintaining familiar routines helps reduce confusion. Use visual or written guides to communicate steps clearly, involve trusted caregivers in planning, and have calming objects or sensory tools on hand to help manage stress.

MENTAL HEALTH CONSIDERATIONS

Floods often exacerbate anxiety or trauma responses. Ensure emergency medications are accessible and provide quiet spaces to help calm distress. Minimizing loud noises and bright lights can reduce overstimulation during crises.

FEMA suggests creating a disability resource. It should include essential medical information, emergency contacts, care instructions, and visual symbols to assist first responders. Every at-risk individual should have a waterproof, printed copy readily available.

For communication, people who are nonverbal or who rely on assistive technology should ensure devices like text-to-speech tablets are charged and included in their emergency kits. Dry-erase boards or notepads offer simple, reliable alternatives. Phones should be preloaded with emergency contacts and placed somewhere easily accessible.

Clear identification is essential in chaotic environments. Wearing a lanyard or wristband with medical details and instructions can help responders act quickly and appropriately. Color-coded communication cards with simple messages such as "I need help" or "I am okay" allow for rapid, nonverbal communication.

Prepared flashcards that describe medical needs or preferred assistance methods can also be lifesaving. Cards might say, "I am nonverbal," or "I need my service animal," along with directions like "Lift me by the straps under my arms." To signal for help, devices such as flashing lightsticks, whistles, or hand-crank lanterns, which are particularly effective in low visibility or noisy settings, should be carried.

Homes can be modified to better withstand flood conditions. Installing grab bars, using nonslip flooring, and placing lighting at floor level help maintain safe movement during power loss or water intrusion. Power cords and medical equipment should be elevated off the floor whenever possible.

Community-wide preparedness also matters. Participating in inclusive evacuation drills ensures dependents and their caregivers are familiar with accessible routes, the use of ramps or evacuation sleds, and the layout of nearby shelters.

Ultimately, flood preparedness must be rooted in equity and inclusion. Addressing the needs of people with disabilities is not optional, it is central to public health and emergency safety. Governments must ensure shelters and protocols are truly accessible. Families and caregivers must build these considerations into their emergency plans. And anyone with vulnerabilities should be equipped with the tools, training, and confidence to act when disaster strikes.

PET SAFETY

Pets are cherished members of the family. In times of crisis, such as during a flood, ensuring the safety of animals is not only a moral obligation but also a practical one. Pets not accounted for in emergency plans can delay evacuation and cause owners to attempt rescues under hazardous conditions. Conversely, a well-prepared pet safety plan supports quicker, calmer evacuations and mitigates the likelihood of loss, injury, or separation.

KEEPING PETS CALM AND SECURE

Animals are highly sensitive to environmental changes. Loud noises, unusual smells, water intrusion, and human stress levels can trigger anxiety and erratic behavior in pets. This makes it crucial to establish routines and safety measures that help animals remain calm and controlled before and during a flood.

Pets often perceive danger before humans recognize it. Changes in barometric pressure and shifts in household energy can all contribute to heightened animal stress, even before the first drop of rain falls. Signs of stress include:

- Pacing or restlessness
- Hiding or cowering
- Excessive vocalization (barking, whining, meowing)
- Aggression or clinginess
- Inappropriate elimination (urinating or defecating indoors)

Calming strategies begin long before an emergency and should be practiced regularly.

STRATEGIES TO KEEP PETS CALM

Keeping pets emotionally stable during a flood requires preparation, empathy, and a calm environment. Animals are highly sensitive to changes in their surroundings and the behavior of their humans, so even small efforts can significantly reduce their stress levels.

It's essential to establish a designated safe space in your home where your pet feels secure. This might be a crate, carrier, or a quiet room. Well before any flood threat arises, train your pet to associate this area with comfort and safety. Use positive reinforcement, such as treats, affection, and praise, when they voluntarily enter or rest there. Adding familiar bedding, toys, or a piece of clothing that smells like you can greatly ease anxiety during a crisis.

Pets often mirror human emotions. If you remain calm and speak in a soothing tone, your pets are more likely to stay relaxed. Even if you're feeling stressed, maintaining a steady demeanor can make a significant difference in how your pet copes.

You can also consider using calming aids, but these should be introduced with professional guidance. Products like Thundershirts apply gentle, constant pressure to simulate swaddling, which many animals find comforting. Pheromone sprays, such as Adaptil for dogs or Feliway for cats, replicate natural scents that signal safety. In some cases, CBD oils or calming supplements may be beneficial, but consult a veterinarian prior to use. For pets with severe anxiety, prescribed sedatives may be necessary (again, under strict veterinary supervision and only as a last resort).

During the actual flood event, it's crucial to minimize your pet's exposure to panic-inducing stimuli. Keep them indoors and away from windows, loud noises, or flashing lights. If using a crate or carrier, consider draping it with a breathable blanket to create a den-like environment. Soft music or white noise machines can mask unsettling sounds and provide a soothing atmosphere.

Experiences during the 2019 Mississippi River floods revealed that animals sheltered close to their owners, even in crowded environments, showed fewer signs of distress and illness. Those separated or housed in chaotic, unfamiliar spaces often developed stress-related issues like vomiting or skin irritation.

In every stage of flood preparedness, pets must be considered full members of the household. Their physical safety is vital, but so is their emotional well-being. A calm, well-prepared pet is easier to manage in emergencies and it is more likely to survive with minimal trauma.

WHAT TO PACK IN AN EMERGENCY KIT FOR PETS

Much like humans, pets require essential supplies to survive and stay healthy during and after a disaster. A well-stocked, waterproof pet emergency kit should be packed in advance and stored with your human go-bag or in a place that's easily reachable during evacuation.

1. FOOD AND WATER (MINIMUM 3–7 DAYS' SUPPLY)

❍ Dry kibble stored in airtight, waterproof containers
❍ Canned food with a manual can opener
❍ Collapsible food and water bowls
❍ Rotate food and water every six months

2. MEDICATIONS AND MEDICAL RECORDS

❍ A two-week supply of prescription medications
❍ Printed vet records and vaccination documentation, especially rabies certification
❍ First-aid supplies: tweezers, antiseptic wipes, gauze, gloves, tick remover, and a pet-safe thermometer

3. IDENTIFICATION AND PHOTOS

❍ ID tags securely attached to collars or harnesses
❍ Microchip registration details, including manufacturer and contact info
❍ Printed recent photographs of you with your pet (for proof of ownership if separated)

4. COMFORT AND RESTRAINT TOOLS

- ❍ Extra leash, collar, and harness
- ❍ Muzzle (some shelters may require it for certain dog breeds)
- ❍ Familiar toy or blanket to reduce anxiety
- ❍ Pet carrier or crate labeled with your contact info and marked "Live Animal"

5. SANITATION SUPPLIES

- ❍ Waste bags or litter and disposable trays
- ❍ Paper towels, pet shampoo wipes, and disinfectants
- ❍ Pee pads for dogs or small animals

6. SPECIES-SPECIFIC ITEMS

- ❍ For cats: litter, scoop, hard carrier
- ❍ For small mammals: cage bedding, water bottle, hay, or pellets
- ❍ For birds: cage, food, water dispensers, and a cover to keep them calm
- ❍ For reptiles: heating pads (battery-powered), feeding tongs, special dietary needs

---

HOW TO HANDLE PET EVACUATION AND TEMPORARY SHELTERING

Evacuating with pets adds layers of complexity, especially in scenarios where time is limited and transport options are constrained. Yet, leaving pets behind during a flood can result in suffering, loss, and even death. It's also important to note that many animals left during disasters later pose hazards to rescue teams and public health.

DO NOT LEAVE PETS BEHIND: Even if you believe floodwaters will not reach your home, conditions can change rapidly. Abandoned pets may drown, escape in panic, or die from exposure. In Hurricane Harvey, over 100,000 pets were displaced or perished after being left behind, many because owners believed they'd only be gone a short time.

USE CRATES OR CARRIERS: Loose animals can bolt from fear or be injured in transit. Secure your pet in a crate or carrier, or restrain them in your car with a seatbelt harness. This ensures their safety and prevents distractions while driving.

KNOW PET-FRIENDLY EVACUATION ROUTES AND SHELTERS: Identify and plan to use shelters that allow pets. Many emergency shelters do not admit animals due to allergies, space, or liability, unless they are service animals. Use tools like:

- **Pet-Friendly Shelter Locators:** Services provided by FEMA, the ASPCA, or local animal welfare groups.
- **Local Agreements:** Know which hotels or community centers in your evacuation zone accept pets during emergencies. Prearranged bookings may be a lifesaver.

LABEL AND TAG EVERYTHING: Mark your pet's carrier with your name, phone number, pet's name, and any medical needs. Attach these details with waterproof tags or permanent markers.

USE A "TWO IS ONE, ONE IS NONE" PHILOSOPHY: Keep backups of the essentials (leashes, water bowls, food) in case your primary kit is lost or inaccessible.

MAINTAIN ROUTINE: Stick to familiar feeding, walking, and sleeping schedules. Structure helps animals adapt to temporary environments.

LIMIT INTERACTION WITH OTHER ANIMALS: Even social pets may become territorial or defensive under stress. Avoid forced introductions, and always ask before letting your pet interact with another.

HYGIENE MATTERS: Clean up immediately after your pet, and keep your designated area clean. This improves conditions for everyone and helps ensure pets continue to be welcome.

COMMUNICATE WITH SHELTER STAFF: Notify shelter coordinators of any special needs your pet may have, such as medical conditions, behavioral traits, or required medications.

LONG-TERM DISPLACEMENT

If flooding results in prolonged displacement, explore temporary fostering arrangements through local humane societies, rescue organizations, or veterinary offices. These networks often coordinate with displaced families to house pets until they can be safely reunited.

Pets depend entirely on humans for their safety in a disaster. In the context of floods, where waters rise swiftly and unpredictably, preparation is both a logistical and ethical responsibility. A pet that is calm, properly restrained, and well cared for can survive the chaos much more safely and confidently. This will provide comfort not just to themselves, but to their human companions as well.

Pet preparedness is not an afterthought, it's integral to whole-family readiness. Including pets in drills, stocking species-appropriate supplies, and knowing your evacuation options empower you to act swiftly and compassionately when it matters most.

COMMUNICATION AND SEEKING HELP

Floods often disrupt the very communication systems we depend on: cell towers may go offline, radio signals may weaken, and power outages can render devices useless. Despite these challenges, there are proven strategies for staying informed and successfully interacting with emergency personnel.

THE EMERGENCY ALERT SYSTEM (EAS) AND WIRELESS EMERGENCY ALERTS (WEA)

The United States utilizes the Emergency Alert System (EAS) and Wireless Emergency Alerts (WEA) to disseminate official notifications. These alerts are broadcast on radio, television, and to mobile phones without needing any app or subscription.

- **EAS Alerts:** Usually preempt regular programming on AM/FM radio and television.
- **WEA Alerts:** Appear as text messages on your mobile device, accompanied by a unique tone and vibration.

These systems issue:

- Flash flood warnings
- Evacuation orders
- Shelter-in-place directives
- Amber Alerts and other public safety notifications

To receive them:

- Enable location services and emergency alerts in your phone settings.
- Keep your device charged or backed up with a portable power source.

KNOWING WHEN TO CALL FOR HELP AND WHAT INFORMATION TO PROVIDE

In a flood emergency, it's crucial to understand when to seek immediate help and how to communicate effectively. Emergency services are often overwhelmed during disasters, so knowing how and when to reach out can directly affect how quickly and accurately help arrives.

You should call 911 only in situations where there is an immediate threat to life. This includes rising water entering your home, people trapped in vehicles or buildings, medical emergencies, or any situation where someone is injured or in imminent danger. Fires, severe injuries, or someone experiencing a medical episode are also valid reasons to make an emergency call.

However, not every issue requires 911. You should avoid calling emergency services for updates on the weather, road conditions, or to report a power outage unless it is creating a direct hazard. Nonurgent rescue requests or logistical concerns, such as needing transportation once floodwaters have receded, should be directed to nonemergency numbers like 311 or local flood information hotlines. These resources are specifically designed to handle lower-priority but still-important needs without tying up emergency responders.

When you do need to call for help, be as clear and efficient as possible. Start by giving your exact location. This could be your full address, GPS coordinates, or if you are uncertain, recognizable nearby landmarks. Clearly explain what is happening, such as water rising quickly, someone unable to move without assistance, or someone with a medical condition that complicates evacuation. Include how many people and animals are with you, and mention any disabilities or needs, such as mobility aids or medication requirements. If your phone battery is low, let them know and, if possible, provide an alternate contact method or backup phone number.

Staying calm helps dispatchers process your information faster and give you the right instructions.

- Speak slowly and deliberately, especially when explaining your needs.
- Avoid shouting unless necessary.
- Practice active listening: Repeat what you hear back to confirm understanding.

If a voice call doesn't go through or if you can't speak, try texting 911. Many areas now support this service. Keep messages brief and to the point: write who you are, where you are, what is happening, and who is with you.

HOW TO SIGNAL FOR HELP IF YOU'RE TRAPPED OR IN DANGER

When communication systems fail, whether due to signal loss, physical injury, or damaged equipment, visual and auditory signals become your lifeline to rescue. These methods can alert first responders or passersby to your location, even when you're unable to speak or move freely.

VISUAL SIGNALS

In addition to using bright colors or a flashlight at night to attract attention (see page 125), creating signage can also make a crucial difference. If possible, write the word "HELP" in large, clear letters using chalk, tape, paint, or any contrasting material. The best location is a flat, visible surface, like a rooftop, driveway, or open yard, where aerial teams can easily spot it. During

Hurricane Katrina, many survivors were located only because they marked their homes with large visual distress messages using bedsheets, tarps, or spray paint. Without these, they might have been missed entirely.

In daylight, you can also use reflective surfaces to catch attention. Small mirrors, compact discs, or even shiny cooking utensils can reflect sunlight in flashes that are visible from great distances. Aim them toward helicopters, boats, or elevated points that might be monitored.

AUDITORY SIGNALS

Sound travels farther than you might expect, especially in quiet environments where normal voices are muffled. A whistle is one of the most effective signaling tools, especially when used in a pattern. Blowing three short bursts every 30 seconds is an internationally recognized distress call and should be repeated until help responds. Whistles are compact, require no power, and can be heard over long distances or through debris.

If you don't have a whistle, improvisation is key. Banging on metal pipes, radiators, or walls with a solid object at regular intervals creates a sharp, rhythmic noise that rescuers are trained to listen for. Even tapping on debris or furniture can serve the same purpose if consistent and repeated.

It's a good idea to store whistles in every emergency kit and attach one to your keyring or backpack. Children should also have access to them and be taught how and when to use them, in case they become separated during a crisis.

INTERACTING WITH EMERGENCY RESPONDERS

Emergency responders, such as firefighters, paramedics, police, National Guard, Coast Guard, and volunteer rescue teams, play a vital role during floods. These professionals are trained to operate in hazardous environments, but their efficiency often depends on the cooperation and clarity of communication from civilians.

Emergency responders operate within a chain of command and have to prioritize lives based on urgency and accessibility. If they cannot take everyone in a single trip, they will return. Avoid confrontations, which delay rescue operations.

When emergency responders arrive during a flood, their goal is to evacuate as many people as possible, as safely and efficiently as conditions allow. Your cooperation can make their job easier and significantly increase your chances of a smooth, successful evacuation.

BE READY TO MOVE: As soon as you know that rescue teams may be in your area, begin preparing immediately. Gather all family members, pets, and prepacked emergency bags. Keep everyone dressed in sturdy shoes and weather-appropriate clothing, and move toward a designated exit or the most accessible part of your home. Pets should be leashed or crated well in advance because loose or panicked animals can delay your evacuation or cause injuries.

Stay calm and alert. If you can see or hear rescuers nearby, signal your presence using a flashlight, whistle, or by calling out. Make sure your entire group is visible and ready to go as soon as help arrives.

FOLLOW INSTRUCTIONS PRECISELY: Rescue crews often operate under extreme pressure, navigating floodwaters, debris, and unpredictable conditions. They will issue direct, sometimes urgent instructions, and this is not the time for debate or hesitation. Respond quickly and clearly. If they ask you to leave belongings behind, comply unless the item is essential to health or identity, such as medication, mobility aids, identification, or critical documents.

Let them know immediately if anyone in your group has medical conditions, mobility issues, or disabilities that require assistance. Rescuers need this information to adapt their procedures and ensure everyone's safety, including their own. By being prepared, organized, and responsive, you not only help yourself but also allow rescue teams to move on to help others more quickly. In a crisis where every minute counts, cooperation is appreciated and can save lives.

AFTER RESCUE: Once you've been transported to a shelter, triage site, or other emergency location, the immediate danger may have passed, but important steps remain to ensure your safety and support recovery efforts.

Begin by registering with disaster relief personnel. This step is crucial as it allows emergency services and organizations like the Red Cross or FEMA to track your location and reunite you with separated family members. Many shelters use digital systems or paper forms to log your name, contact details, and any medical needs.

Cooperate fully with intake questions, which may include your recent exposure to floodwaters, any symptoms of illness or injury, and your housing situation. This information helps triage workers and public health officials manage resources and prioritize care.

Once inside, follow all posted rules and verbal instructions from shelter staff. Stay in designated areas to ensure order and safety, especially during high-volume intake periods. Only leave your assigned space if you are instructed to do so or need medical attention.

While shelters aim to provide food, water, and basic necessities, resources may be limited. Patience, cooperation, and kindness toward both staff and fellow evacuees go a long way in helping everyone through the difficult hours and days after a disaster.

COMMUNICATION HUBS

In disaster-prone areas, some communities develop communication hubs that function during system outages:

- **Amateur Radio Networks (HAM):** Certified operators often assist in emergency communications. Local governments sometimes rely on these groups when traditional channels fail.
- **Neighborhood Watch or CERT (Community Emergency Response Teams):** See page 70.

If your area does not yet have such a system, consider joining or forming one. During the 2010 Nashville flood, several communities credited neighborhood response groups for organizing door-to-door rescues and relaying critical information long before official services arrived.

By mastering the use of emergency systems, knowing when and how to request assistance, and understanding what to expect from responders, we can navigate the chaos of a flood with greater clarity and confidence. Clear communication saves lives, reduces fear, and builds the foundation for coordinated recovery.

DEALING WITH FEAR AND ANXIETY

While many preparedness resources focus on logistics (what to pack, when to evacuate, how to communicate), few address the psychological toll that can paralyze even the most physically prepared individual. Understanding and managing fear is as critical to survival as securing food or finding shelter.

TECHNIQUES FOR MANAGING FEAR DURING A CRISIS

Fear is a natural biological response to danger. When faced with a threat, the body initiates the "fight, flight, or freeze" response, releasing adrenaline, increasing heart rate, and sharpening focus. While this reaction can be lifesaving in some situations, unchecked fear often leads to:

- Panic and irrational decisions
- Miscommunication
- Physical symptoms like hyperventilation or fainting
- Frozen inaction, even when movement is essential

In flood scenarios, these responses can be especially hazardous. Running into floodwaters, refusing evacuation, or forgetting essential supplies are just a few examples of poor decisions rooted in unmanaged fear. Recognizing fear as a physiological reaction and learning how to regulate it is essential.

Managing fear during a flood or other high-stress emergency isn't about suppressing emotions. It's about redirecting them into useful actions that can be mirrored by others. Regulating your emotions can help you think clearly, make lifesaving decisions, and support others. Here's how to maintain composure and focus under pressure.

MINDFULNESS TECHNIQUES

POSITIVE SELF-TALK AND VISUALIZATION

What you tell yourself during a crisis has real consequences. Thoughts like "We're doomed" can trigger helplessness and paralysis. Replace those with affirmations such as, "I can take the next right step," or "I have done hard things before." Visualization also helps. Imagine each step of staying safe, whether it's gathering supplies, moving to higher ground, or calling for help. Mental rehearsal strengthens the same pathways in the brain used for action, making it easier to follow through when the moment arrives.

FOCUS ON ACTIONABLE TASKS

Anxiety thrives in moments of helplessness. One of the fastest ways to break through fear is to take clear, purposeful action. Start small. Locate your flashlight, text a loved one your status, fill a water bottle, or double-check your go-bag. Each small task reinforces a sense of control and forward motion. During the 2018 Kerala floods, survivors often cited their ability to stay focused on helping others by preparing food, caring for pets, or organizing supplies. It became key to managing their own fears.

PRAYER, MEDITATION, AND RITUAL

For those with spiritual beliefs, prayer or familiar rituals can offer profound comfort during uncertain times. Even nonreligious forms of meditation, such as repeating a calming phrase, visualizing a peaceful place, or focusing on the rhythm of your breath, can reduce distress and provide mental shelter in moments of overwhelm.

SUPPORTING OTHERS THROUGH PANIC

In every emergency, there will be people who panic, as children, neighbors, and even strong adults can be suddenly overwhelmed. Being able to support someone else emotionally is just as vital as providing food or shelter. It stabilizes your group and prevents bad decisions driven by fear.

VALIDATE EMOTIONS

Avoid saying things like “Calm down” or “There’s nothing to worry about.” These phrases often backfire. Instead, acknowledge the emotion and offer support: “It’s okay to be scared. I’m scared too, but we’ll get through this.” A simple statement of shared experience can defuse the intensity of someone’s panic and help them reengage with reality.

USE A CALM, STEADY TONE

We naturally mirror the emotions we see. If you speak slowly, clearly, and with grounded body language (steady hands, eye contact, and calm tone and pacing) others will begin to regulate themselves in response. This process is called co-regulation, and it’s a powerful emotional tool in group dynamics.

GIVE SIMPLE, CLEAR INSTRUCTIONS

When someone is overwhelmed, they can’t process complex steps. Give one directive at a time: “Put your coat on,” or “We’re walking to the car now.” Whenever possible, pair words with gentle physical guidance by placing the item in their hands, pointing to a path, or taking their hand to lead them.

ASSIGN SMALL, MEANINGFUL TASKS

Giving someone a role, no matter how small, redirects their brain from panic to purpose. Ask them to count bags, check on a pet, or hold a flashlight. Children especially benefit from this approach. During the 2022 Kentucky floods, many parents found their children calmed quickly when they were asked to help collect items or care for pets.

USE PHYSICAL REASSURANCE WITH CONSENT

Touch can be very calming and welcomed during stressful times. Holding hands, placing a hand on the back, or offering a hug may help loved ones feel secure. However, always consider personal boundaries, past trauma, or cultural norms. Never assume touch is comforting unless you know the person well or they initiate it.

SPECIAL CONSIDERATIONS

FOR CHILDREN: Children sense emotional cues from adults. If caregivers show calm, children will feel safer, even if they don't fully understand what's happening. Use simple explanations: "The water is outside, but we're safe in here." Establish routines such as regular meals, quiet playtime, or stories to give them a sense of predictability. Let them draw, talk, or act out their fears. This is how many children process distress.

FOR THE ELDERLY: Older adults may hide their distress or become disoriented in a crisis, particularly if they have dementia or other cognitive impairments. Speak slowly, offer reassurance, and repeat instructions as needed. Familiar items such as photos, blankets, or mementos can help ground them emotionally and cognitively.

FOR PEOPLE WITH DISABILITIES: Support should be tailored to the person's unique needs. Those with autism, sensory sensitivities, or communication challenges may need headphones, weighted blankets, or visual aids. Keep communication cards or assistive devices accessible, and respect their known calming strategies.

MANAGING EMOTIONAL FALLOUT AFTER THE IMMEDIATE CRISIS

Fear is a universal response to disaster, but it doesn't have to be a paralyzing one. Through simple, evidence-based strategies like grounding, controlled breathing, and calm leadership, you can manage your emotional response and help others do the same. Fear doesn't end when the waters recede. Survivors may face post-traumatic stress, grief, survivor's guilt, and ongoing anxiety, especially if homes, pets, or loved ones were lost.

Here are some ways to provide post-flood emotional first aid:

- Talk about the experience with trusted friends or professionals.
- Reestablish routines and control where possible.
- Limit constant media exposure about the disaster.
- Seek counseling if symptoms persist (nightmares, detachment, excessive vigilance).

Organizations such as the Red Cross, FEMA, and local mental health agencies often provide post-disaster emotional support services.

In the context of a flood, where decisions must be made quickly and lives depend on composure, emotional readiness is a survival tool. Preparing for the psychological side of disaster may not be as visible as sandbags or flashlights, but it is just as essential. Understanding how fear works, and practicing ways to manage it, ensures that when the storm comes, you can act with clarity and compassion, not only for yourself but for those who depend on you.

CHAPTER 6

AFTER THE FLOOD: RECOVERY AND RESTORATION

Returning to your home after a flood marks a critical phase in the recovery process. While the immediate threat of rising waters may have passed, the aftermath presents a host of new risks, such as structural damage, compromised utilities, hazardous contaminants, and sanitation concerns, all of which demand careful attention. For those committed to safety, understanding how to accurately assess the condition of their homes and implement necessary precautions is paramount.

ASSESSING STRUCTURAL SAFETY: THE FOUNDATION OF A SAFE RETURN

Before stepping through the threshold, the first and foremost consideration must be whether the building is structurally sound. Floodwaters can erode soil supporting foundations, weaken load-bearing walls, and compromise key structural elements, such as floors, beams, and roof supports.

VISUAL AND PHYSICAL INSPECTION: A preliminary external inspection can offer vital clues. Look for visible signs such as leaning walls, cracks in the foundation, sagging roofs, or doors and windows that no longer fit their frames correctly. If floodwaters have been particularly high or persistent, as seen in the catastrophic flooding of Hurricane Harvey, many homes will exhibit foundational washouts and severe structural undermining. Local authorities often advise that if there is any visible sign of structural damage, entry should be deferred until a qualified structural engineer or building inspector can conduct a formal assessment.

PROFESSIONAL STRUCTURAL EVALUATION: In many instances, homeowners may not be able to accurately gauge the extent of damage without expert input. Structural engineers use specialized tools and methods, such as infrared imaging, moisture meters, and load-bearing assessments, to evaluate compromised areas that may not be visible to the naked eye. For example, after the 2010–2011 Queensland floods in Australia, extensive inspections revealed numerous homes with hidden mold growth inside wall cavities and weakened timber frames, which could have led to collapse if left unaddressed.

FOUNDATION AND FLOOR STABILITY: Floodwaters often saturate soil beneath the foundation, causing subsidence or heaving. If floors feel spongy or uneven, or if there are creaking noises when walking, these can be signs of compromised subfloor structures. Additionally, waterlogged materials may lose their integrity. Concrete slabs might crack under pressure, and wood framing can rot quickly if left wet for extended periods.

IDENTIFYING GAS LEAKS AND OTHER UTILITY HAZARDS

Utilities pose immediate, life-threatening risks in flood-damaged homes. Gas leaks, electrical shorts, and water-contaminated plumbing require meticulous scrutiny before restoring normal occupancy.

NATURAL GAS AND PROPANE SAFETY: Flooding can dislodge gas lines, damage connections, or corrode valves, leading to leaks that risk explosions or carbon monoxide poisoning. After Hurricane Katrina, numerous cases of gas leaks caused fires and fatalities when residents returned prematurely to damaged homes. The standard protocol is to ensure that the gas supply has been shut off at the main valve by a qualified technician before entering. If you smell gas (characterized by a distinctive sulfur-like odor) or hear hissing sounds, evacuate immediately and contact emergency services.

Even if no gas is detected, professional inspection is required before restoring supply. Utility companies often perform leak tests and pressure checks to certify safety.

ELECTRICAL HAZARDS: Water and electricity are a dangerous combination. Standing water within homes can energize outlets, appliances, and wiring, leading to electrocution risks. It is crucial that electrical power remains off at the main breaker before anyone enters a flooded building. Homeowners should never attempt to restore power themselves but rather wait for a licensed electrician to inspect and certify that circuits and devices are safe.

After flooding in the Midwest from the Great Flood of the Mississippi River in 1993, many injuries and fatalities were linked to live wires submerged or damp wiring causing short circuits. Outlets and breakers should be checked for water intrusion, and all electrical appliances that were submerged must be replaced or professionally evaluated.

WATER SUPPLY AND SEWAGE: Floodwaters often contaminate potable water lines, leading to bacterial and chemical hazards. Likewise, sewage systems can back up, causing health risks from exposure to pathogens. It is essential to have the water supply tested before use, and any private wells must be disinfected following protocols recommended by health departments and the CDC.

PRECAUTIONS WHEN ENTERING A FLOODED AREA: PROTECTIVE GEAR AND SANITATION

Entering a home or area affected by flooding requires proper protective measures to reduce risks of injury, infection, and exposure to hazardous materials.

PERSONAL PROTECTIVE EQUIPMENT (PPE): Due to the multiple hazards present in flood-impacted homes, including sharp debris, contaminated water, mold spores, and chemicals, wearing appropriate PPE should be mandatory. This includes sturdy waterproof boots or waders, gloves made of nitrile or heavy rubber, long-sleeved shirts and pants to minimize skin contact, and safety goggles or face shields to protect against splashes.

Respiratory protection is crucial, especially when disturbing mold or debris. N95 respirators or higher-grade masks prevent inhalation of harmful particulates. For instance, in the aftermath of Hurricane Sandy, widespread mold contamination necessitated the use of respirators during cleanup to prevent respiratory illnesses.

SANITATION CONCERNS: Floodwaters often carry a cocktail of biological and chemical contaminants (sewage, pesticides, fuel, heavy metals, and other pollutants) that can cause serious health problems. It is important to avoid ingesting or coming into contact with floodwater. Washing hands frequently, especially before eating or touching your face, is critical.

Standing water left in homes encourages the proliferation of bacteria and mold, which pose respiratory and allergic risks. Areas with visible mold must be handled carefully, and those with preexisting respiratory conditions or immunocompromised states should avoid entering until professional remediation is complete.

DEBRIS AND SHARP OBJECTS: Floodwaters often deposit debris such as broken glass, rusted metal, and wood splinters. Even if the water has receded, floors and yards may still conceal these hazards. Walking carefully, using a flashlight to inspect dark areas, and avoiding bare feet reduce injury risks.

PSYCHOLOGICAL AND EMOTIONAL CONSIDERATIONS UPON REENTRY

While this section focuses on physical safety, it is important to acknowledge the emotional toll associated with returning to a flood-damaged home.

Many homeowners report feelings of shock, loss, and anxiety when confronting the scale of destruction.

Preparedness for the emotional impact includes bringing support persons, allowing time to rest and recover, and contacting mental health professionals if feelings of overwhelm persist.

The process of returning home after a flood is fraught with hazards but, with appropriate caution, knowledge, and support, you can protect yourself, your family, and your property during this critical phase. Next, we will explore the steps involved in cleanup, remediation, and rebuilding to restore homes and lives with resilience.

WATER DAMAGE MITIGATION

Ensuing moisture triggers a cascade of secondary problems, including structural deterioration, mold growth, and long-term material degradation. Effective water damage mitigation is essential to halt this progression, preserve the integrity of the home, and safeguard the health of its occupants.

The primary objective following a flood is to remove standing water as swiftly and safely as possible. Prolonged saturation accelerates damage to building materials and furnishings and creates optimal conditions for microbial growth.

PUMPING OUT WATER: If floodwaters remain inside the structure, controlled pumping is the first step. This task requires careful attention to the building's structural status. Removing water too rapidly can cause pressure imbalances that further damage foundations or walls. This is a phenomenon observed in many flood events, including the catastrophic 2010 Pakistan floods, where hastily drained homes experienced wall collapse.

Professional water removal services employ submersible pumps and vacuums suited to the volume and location of water. When doing it yourself, use portable pumps or wet/dry vacuums, but only if you are confident that the building is structurally safe and that utilities (electricity and gas) are properly shut off or restored under supervision.

REMOVAL OF WET MATERIALS: Materials that cannot be dried quickly or thoroughly should be removed to prevent further damage and mold growth. This includes carpets, padding, upholstered furniture, drywall, insulation, and sometimes wooden flooring. According to the EPA, drywall soaked for more than 24-48 hours should be discarded, as it often becomes a breeding ground for mold.

In cases where valuable or historic materials are involved, specialized drying and restoration services may employ techniques such as vacuum freeze-drying or controlled dehumidification to salvage materials.

DRYING OUT YOUR HOME: TOOLS AND TECHNIQUES

After initial water removal and removal of saturated materials, drying out the home effectively is the next critical step. This phase requires mechanical assistance to reduce humidity and moisture content in the structure and remaining contents.

DEHUMIDIFIERS: Dehumidifiers extract moisture from the air, speeding the drying of walls, floors, and furniture. Two primary types are used in flood restoration:

- **Refrigerant Dehumidifiers:** These work by cooling air below its dew point, condensing moisture, and collecting water in tanks or drainage systems. They are effective in moderate to warm environments and are often employed in typical residential settings.
- **Desiccant Dehumidifiers:** Using a moisture-absorbing material, these are effective in colder environments or areas where refrigerant dehumidifiers are less efficient.

The strategic placement of dehumidifiers is vital. Position them centrally within rooms and near remaining wet surfaces. Larger spaces or heavily saturated areas may require multiple units. Professionals often monitor humidity levels with hygrometers to track progress and adjust equipment placement.

FANS AND AIR CIRCULATION: Fans complement dehumidifiers by circulating air, enhancing evaporation from wet surfaces. High-velocity fans or axial blowers are typically employed to move large volumes of air.

However, take care to avoid blowing air directly onto mold spores or contaminated materials without filtration, as this can spread contaminants. Negative air machines equipped with HEPA filters are used in professional remediation to contain and capture airborne mold spores.

VENTILATION: Natural ventilation, where safe and practical, assists drying by introducing fresh air. Opening windows and doors, weather permitting, facilitates evaporation. However, this method depends on favorable weather and outdoor air quality.

TEMPERATURE CONTROL: Maintaining moderate warmth (around 70 to 80°F or 21 to 27°C) during drying accelerates evaporation and inhibits mold growth. Heating systems may be used carefully, ensuring they do not add humidity.

MONITORING AND MANAGING MOISTURE LEVELS

Drying is a gradual process and must be monitored to ensure thoroughness. Moisture meters, infrared cameras, and hygrometers enable the detection of hidden wet spots in walls, floors, and cavities.

Many homeowners underestimate moisture retention in cavities behind drywall or within flooring layers, which, if overlooked, can cause recurrent mold outbreaks and structural deterioration.

The Institute of Inspection Cleaning and Restoration Certification emphasizes that drying times vary based on building materials, climate, and the extent of saturation, but thorough drying can take several days to weeks.

DISPOSAL OF CONTAMINATED MATERIALS

Materials exposed to floodwaters, including carpets, drywall, insulation, and personal belongings, may be classified as hazardous waste and must be disposed of according to local regulations.

Use of biocides or antimicrobial treatments is common after removal of wet materials to inhibit microbial growth. However, these treatments are most effective when combined with thorough drying.

Licensed waste disposal services ensure compliance and safety. Failure to properly dispose of contaminated materials risks prolonged health hazards and environmental contamination.

IDENTIFYING MOLD AND UNDERSTANDING ITS HEALTH RISKS

Mold is a form of fungus that thrives in moist, warm environments. It can appear in damp environments in 24 to 48 hours, only requiring moisture and organic material to flourish. Common species found in flood-damaged homes include *Stachybotrys chartarum* (black mold), *Aspergillus, Penicillium,* and *Cladosporium.* Visually, mold may appear as fuzzy or slimy patches ranging in color from black, green, or gray to white or orange. These colonies can develop on drywall, wood, carpeting, insulation, and even beneath surfaces like wallpaper.

Mold can produce a musty odor, often the first indicator of hidden growth behind walls or under floors. It is critical to distinguish mold growth from dirt or staining, as the former poses significant risks.

HEALTH RISKS: Exposure to mold spores and fragments can trigger a wide spectrum of health effects, particularly for vulnerable groups, including children, the elderly, people with asthma or allergies, and those with weakened immune systems. According to the CDC, mold exposure can cause:

- Respiratory symptoms like coughing, wheezing, nasal congestion, and throat irritation
- Allergic reactions like sneezing, red eyes, and skin rash
- Increased frequency and severity of asthma attacks
- In rare cases, invasive fungal infections in immunocompromised individuals

The toxicity of molds like *Stachybotrys* is still being studied, but prolonged exposure to dense colonies may increase the risk of more severe respiratory conditions.

SAFE AND EFFECTIVE MOLD REMOVAL TECHNIQUES

Mold remediation after flooding is both an urgent and delicate task. Proper removal requires controlling spore dispersal, protecting the cleanup crew, and eliminating mold from all affected surfaces.

PERSONAL PROTECTIVE EQUIPMENT: Anyone engaging in mold cleanup should wear appropriate PPE, including N95 or higher-grade respirators, gloves, goggles, and protective clothing. This prevents inhalation of spores and skin contact with potentially toxic substances.

CONTAINMENT: To limit the spread of spores, affected areas should be isolated using plastic sheeting and negative air pressure devices if possible. Doors and vents should be sealed to prevent contamination of unaffected areas.

SMALL-SCALE REMEDIATION: For minor mold infestations (typically under 10 square feet), homeowners may clean surfaces with detergent and water followed by disinfection with a solution such as diluted bleach (one cup bleach per gallon of water). It is important to never mix bleach with ammonia or other cleaners, as doing so can produce harmful fumes.

Porous materials that are heavily contaminated, such as drywall, insulation, and carpet padding, generally cannot be cleaned effectively and must be discarded. After removal, the underlying areas should be dried thoroughly and cleaned.

NONPOROUS SURFACES: Hard surfaces such as glass, metal, and plastic can be cleaned and disinfected more readily. After mold removal, surfaces should be monitored for recurrence.

AVOID DRY SCRAPING OR SANDING: These actions disturb mold spores and increase airborne contamination. Instead, wet methods or HEPA-filtered vacuuming are preferred to minimize spore dispersal.

WHEN TO HIRE A PROFESSIONAL

Professional mold remediation is strongly recommended when:

- Mold growth exceeds 10 square feet
- Mold has penetrated heating, ventilation, and air conditioning (HVAC) systems
- The infestation is caused by contaminated water such as sewage or chemical-laden floodwaters
- Occupants have significant health issues or sensitivities
- Mold has penetrated structural elements or is hidden in inaccessible areas (e.g., inside walls or under floors)

Certified mold remediation specialists use specialized equipment such as HEPA air scrubbers, industrial vacuums, antimicrobial treatments, and containment chambers to safely and effectively remove mold. They also provide clearance testing to verify that mold levels have returned to safe limits.

PREVENTIVE MEASURES TO AVOID MOLD RECURRENCE

Preventing mold after flooding hinges on the following moisture-control measures:

- Dry the structure completely within 24 to 48 hours.
- Repair leaks and address drainage issues around the home.
- Maintain indoor humidity levels below 60 percent, ideally between 30 percent and 50 percent.
- Use dehumidifiers and ventilation effectively during and after cleanup.
- Discard water-damaged porous materials that cannot be fully dried.

- Apply mold inhibitors or antimicrobial treatments to vulnerable surfaces.

Ongoing vigilance is necessary. Regular inspections, especially in basements, crawl spaces, and attics, help identify early signs of moisture and mold before they become major problems.

By integrating these practices into flood recovery plans, homeowners and communities can reduce the long-term consequences of flooding, ensuring a safer, healthier return to normal life.

APPEALING DENIED OR INADEQUATE CLAIMS

If a claim is denied or compensation seems insufficient, review your policy carefully. Seek assistance from your state's insurance commissioner, consumer protection agencies, or a qualified attorney specializing in insurance disputes.

APPLYING FOR GOVERNMENT AID AND DISASTER RELIEF PROGRAMS

In large-scale flooding events, government agencies often provide supplemental assistance to affected individuals and communities. These programs can help bridge gaps in insurance coverage and support recovery efforts.

FEDERAL DISASTER ASSISTANCE: In the US, FEMA administers disaster aid after a presidential declaration. Aid can include grants for temporary housing, home repairs, low-interest disaster loans through the Small Business Administration, and crisis counseling.

To apply, register online or via phone as soon as possible. FEMA inspectors will visit to assess damages and verify eligibility. Documentation requirements mirror those for insurance claims, emphasizing the importance of thorough record-keeping.

STATE AND LOCAL PROGRAMS: Many states and municipalities offer additional programs, such as emergency rental assistance, rebuilding grants, or tax relief. These vary by jurisdiction and event severity.

NONGOVERNMENTAL ORGANIZATIONS: Organizations such as the Red Cross, Salvation Army, and local charities provide immediate relief supplies, temporary shelter, and sometimes financial aid or rebuilding assistance.

ELIGIBILITY AND COORDINATION: It is important to note that government aid typically requires that applicants pursue all available insurance claims first, to avoid duplication of benefits. Coordination between insurers and aid agencies is common to ensure efficient distribution of resources.

Financial recovery after flooding is a multifaceted process involving meticulous damage documentation, careful navigation of insurance claims, and strategic utilization of government and charitable aid. Preparation, prompt action, and persistence are critical to securing the funds necessary for rebuilding and returning to normalcy.

Homeowners who proactively document losses, understand their insurance policies, and engage fully with both insurers and aid programs improve their chances of a successful financial recovery. This financial stability is a cornerstone of resilient flood recovery.

CONCLUSION

PREPARING TODAY FOR A SAFER TOMORROW

As we draw this handbook to a close, it's vital to reflect on the central message threading through every chapter: proactive planning and informed preparation are the most powerful defenses against flooding and water-related disasters. Floods and hurricanes are increasing in frequency and intensity, fueled by climate change, population growth in vulnerable areas, and aging infrastructure. Yet, with knowledge, foresight, and community effort, we can significantly reduce risks to our homes, families, and livelihoods.

This final chapter revisits the critical importance of staying informed and prepared for future risks and underscores the collective responsibility to build a flood-safe culture within our communities. These efforts not only protect individual households but also strengthen resilience at the neighborhood, city, and regional levels.

THE IMPORTANCE OF PROACTIVE PLANNING

Floods rarely come with ample warning, and their impacts can be sudden and devastating. While it's impossible to control the weather, you can control how prepared you are before the waters rise. Proactive planning means anticipating potential dangers and putting preventive measures in place well in advance. This mindset shifts you from reacting in the heat of crisis to responding with calm, effective actions.

Throughout this book, you've learned how to assess flood risks when buying or renting a home. You've learned how to understand flood zones, evaluate foundation safety, and recognize neighborhood preparedness. You've seen how flood insurance works, why it's essential, and how to navigate policies so you're not caught unprotected. You've also gained practical knowledge on utilizing NOAA flood maps and local resources, preparing your home with defensive upgrades, assembling emergency supplies, and planning evacuation or shelter-in-place strategies.

But proactive planning doesn't stop once you've fortified your own home or packed your emergency kit. It requires ongoing vigilance by regularly updating your information, reviewing and revising your plans, and staying connected to community alerts and weather updates.

HOW TO STAY INFORMED AND PREPARED FOR FUTURE RISKS

Staying informed is essential for effective flood preparedness, especially as flood risks evolve over time due to factors like new development, changing waterways, shifting climate patterns, and updated floodplain mapping. To stay ahead of potential threats, it's important to engage in a series of ongoing, proactive measures.

Start by regularly monitoring authoritative sources. Agencies like NOAA and FEMA provide critical updates, including flood maps, weather alerts, and educational materials. Your local government and emergency management offices are also valuable resources, often offering real-time flood warnings, evacuation routes, and public safety alerts. Additionally, subscribing to emergency notifications from the National Weather Service and local agencies, via smartphone apps or emergency radios, can help ensure you receive timely alerts.

Community engagement plays a vital role in preparedness. Join neighborhood watch programs or Community Emergency Response Teams and participate in disaster preparedness workshops or town meetings. Discussing flood history and safety strategies with neighbors helps build a network of awareness and shared readiness.

It's equally important to keep your personal preparedness plans current. Update your emergency kit seasonally, replacing expired items and restocking essentials. Practice evacuation drills with your family, ensuring everyone knows the routes and communication plan. Also, review your flood insurance policy annually to confirm that it accurately reflects any changes in property value or possessions.

Lastly, invest in maintaining and improving your home's defenses. Regularly inspect drainage systems, sump pumps, and flood barriers. If needed, consider elevation projects or floodproofing renovations based on the latest risk assessments. By making these practices part of your routine, you create a lasting and adaptive approach to flood preparedness, transforming it from a one-time task into a lifelong commitment to safety.

BUILDING A FLOOD-SAFE CULTURE IN YOUR COMMUNITY

Individual preparedness is essential, but flooding is a shared risk that requires collective action. Creating a flood-safe culture within your community enhances protection for everyone and encourages cooperation during emergencies.

A strong flood-safe culture begins with awareness and education. Share your knowledge with neighbors, schools, and local organizations. Get involved in or help organize campaigns that promote understanding of flood risks and preparation strategies.

Advocating for stronger local policies is another key step. Work with local government officials to support effective floodplain management, stricter building codes, and urban planning practices that respect natural water flow and drainage patterns.

Community infrastructure improvements play a vital role in reducing flood risks. Support investments in green infrastructure, such as rain gardens, permeable pavements, and wetland restoration, which help absorb and slow runoff. Encourage ongoing maintenance and upgrades to levees, dams, and drainage systems to ensure they function effectively.

Fostering neighborly cooperation strengthens community resilience. Encourage the sharing of resources and information, establish check-in systems for vulnerable residents, coordinate evacuation support, and work together to maintain local flood defenses.

Preparing for collective emergency response is equally important. Join or help create local CERTs to train residents in basic emergency skills. Communities with organized and trained volunteers are better equipped to respond to and recover from flooding events.

THE BROADER IMPACT OF PREPAREDNESS

Flood preparedness goes beyond protecting against physical damage. It also promotes emotional well-being by reducing fear and uncertainty, supports economic stability by limiting financial losses, and safeguards public health by preventing hazards like contaminated water and mold. Moreover, resilient communities attract investment and enjoy higher property values, as safety and sustainability become valued priorities in the real estate market.

FINAL THOUGHTS: YOUR ROLE IN A CHANGING CLIMATE

The challenge posed by floods and hurricanes is part of the larger story of climate change. While governments and scientists work to address global causes, individual and community-level actions remain our frontline defense.

By applying the knowledge from this book, you become a vital part of the solution. Your efforts to choose flood-safe housing, secure insurance, prepare your home and family, respond safely during emergencies, and support recovery contribute to a safer future for all.

Remember, preparation is empowerment. It transforms vulnerability into strength and uncertainty into confidence. The work you do today, which is not just for yourself, but for your community, builds a legacy of resilience that will protect generations to come. May this knowledge serve you well in creating a secure, flood-safe environment where you and your loved ones can thrive, no matter what nature brings.

RESOURCES AND FURTHER READING

For those who want to explore more about flood preparedness, insurance, and recovery, the following resources offer authoritative guidance, tools, and support:

GOVERNMENT AND OFFICIAL AGENCIES

Federal Emergency Management Agency (FEMA)

Website: www.fema.gov

Extensive resources on flood maps, disaster assistance, mitigation grants, and flood insurance through the National Flood Insurance Program (NFIP).

National Oceanic and Atmospheric Administration (NOAA)

Website: www.noaa.gov

Updated flood maps, weather alerts, storm tracking, and climate information.

National Weather Service (NWS)

Website: www.weather.gov

Real-time flood warnings and forecasts for your local area.

FEMA Flood Map Service Center (MSC)

Website: msc.fema.gov

The official source for flood hazard maps and floodplain information.

US Geological Survey (USGS)

Website: www.usgs.gov

Data and tools related to water flow, flood monitoring, and hydrology.

INSURANCE RESOURCES

National Flood Insurance Program (NFIP)

Website: www.floodsmart.gov

Educational materials, flood insurance quotes, and policy information.

Private Flood Insurance Providers

Contact local insurance agents for private flood insurance options that may offer broader coverage or competitive pricing.

Insurance Information Institute (III)

Website: www.iii.org

Comprehensive guides on flood insurance, claims, and coverage.

EMERGENCY PREPAREDNESS AND RECOVERY

American Red Cross

Website: www.redcross.org

Resources on flood safety, emergency kits, sheltering, and first aid.

Ready.gov

Website: www.ready.gov/floods

Federal guide for preparing for floods and other disasters.

Centers for Disease Control and Prevention (CDC)—Flood Safety

Website: www.cdc.gov/disasters/floods

Information on health risks, mold, and sanitation after flooding.

National Safety Council

Website: www.nsc.org

Safety tips and resources for flood and hurricane preparedness.

COMMUNITY AND LOCAL RESOURCES

Local Emergency Management Offices

Contact your city or county emergency management office for local flood alerts, evacuation routes, and community response programs.

Community Emergency Response Teams (CERT)

Website: www.ready.gov/cert

Training and volunteer opportunities to assist your neighborhood during disasters.

Local Libraries and Extension Offices

Often offer workshops, printed materials, and guidance on flood preparedness and recovery.

ONLINE TOOLS AND APPS

FEMA App: Emergency alerts, preparedness tips, and disaster resources on your phone.

NOAA Weather Radar Live: Real-time weather radar with flood warnings.

Flood Warning Information System (FWIS): Localized flood alerts and river gauge readings.

American Red Cross Emergency App: Weather alerts, first aid tips, and shelter locations.

APPENDICES

FLOOD PREPARATION CHEKLIST

1. Assessing Your Flood Risk

❍ Research if your property is in a flood-prone area using FEMA and NOAA flood maps.

❍ Check local flood history and past flood events in your neighborhood.

❍ Identify nearby water sources: rivers, lakes, oceans, drainage systems.

❍ Understand your flood zone designation and base flood elevation (BFE).

❍ Consult with local building officials about floodplain regulations.

❍ Discuss flood risk with neighbors, real estate agents, and local authorities.

2. Preparing Your Home

Structural and Exterior Preparations

❍ Ensure your home foundation is raised above flood levels where possible.

❍ Install flood vents to allow water to flow through crawlspaces.

❍ Use waterproof or flood-resistant materials for walls, floors, and insulation.

❍ Elevate HVAC systems, electrical panels, and utilities above potential flood levels.

- ❍ Secure roofing, doors, and windows to withstand hurricane-force winds.
- ❍ Inspect and clean gutters and storm drains to ensure proper drainage.
- ❍ Install check valves on sewer lines to prevent backup flooding.
- ❍ Build or reinforce levees, berms, or floodwalls if feasible.

Interior Preparations

- ❍ Move valuable furniture, electronics, and important documents to upper floors or elevated areas.
- ❍ Store important documents (insurance policies, IDs, medical records) in waterproof containers or digitally.
- ❍ Prepare waterproof containers for storing valuables and emergency supplies.
- ❍ Install sump pumps with battery backups for basements.
- ❍ Keep sandbags or temporary flood barriers on hand and accessible.

3. Emergency Supplies and Equipment

- ❍ Assemble an emergency supply kit containing at least 72 hours of necessities for each family member:

  - » Bottled water (one gallon per person per day)
  - » Nonperishable food (canned goods, energy bars)
  - » Manual can opener
  - » First-aid kit (bandages, antiseptics, medications)
  - » Prescription medications and copies of prescriptions
  - » Flashlights with extra batteries
  - » Battery-powered or hand-crank radio
  - » Portable phone chargers and power banks
  - » Waterproof clothing and sturdy shoes/boots
  - » Blankets or sleeping bags
  - » Multi-tool or Swiss Army knife
  - » Personal hygiene items (toothbrush, soap, feminine products)
  - » Whistle to signal for help
  - » Local maps and emergency contact information
  - » Cash in small denominations (ATMs may be down)

- » Life jackets or flotation devices if living in a high-risk area
- » Rope and ladders for evacuation or rescue scenarios

❍ Prepare a pet emergency kit with:

- » food
- » water
- » medications
- » leashes
- » carriers
- » sanitation supplies

❍ Keep a vehicle emergency kit with:

- » jumper cables
- » flares
- » blankets
- » tools

4. Insurance and Financial Preparedness

❍ Review your homeowner's insurance policy to confirm it does NOT cover flood damage.

❍ Purchase separate flood insurance through NFIP or a private insurer.

❍ Understand your flood insurance policy terms: coverage limits, deductibles, exclusions.

❍ Inventory all household belongings with photos and detailed descriptions for claims.

❍ Keep copies of insurance policies and inventory in a safe, accessible location.

❍ Familiarize yourself with the flood insurance claims process.

❍ Set aside emergency funds or savings for disaster-related expenses.

❍ Learn about local, state, and federal disaster aid programs and application processes.

5. Developing a Family Emergency Plan

❍ Designate a safe meeting place inside and outside your home.

❍ Identify multiple evacuation routes and practice them.

❍ Plan for pet care and evacuation.

❍ Assign roles and responsibilities to family members.

❍ Establish a communication plan, including local emergency contacts and out-of-area contacts.

❍ Prepare emergency contact cards for each family member.

❍ Teach children how and when to call 911.

❍ Make arrangements for family members with special needs, disabilities, or those requiring elderly care.

❍ Keep a copy of your emergency plan accessible to all family members.

6. Preparing for the Flood Event

❍ Stay updated on weather alerts via NOAA, FEMA, local authorities, and emergency apps.

❍ Secure outdoor items that could float or become projectiles in floodwaters.

❍ Turn off utilities (electricity, gas, water) if instructed or if flooding is imminent.

❍ Fill bathtubs and containers with clean water for sanitation and drinking.

❍ Disconnect electrical appliances to prevent short circuits and fires.

❍ Place sandbags or flood barriers at doors and low windows.

❍ Elevate furniture and valuables or move them to higher floors.

❍ Charge all mobile devices and power banks.

❍ Pack your "go-bag" with essentials, documents, medications, and clothes.

❍ Inform neighbors, especially those who may need assistance.

❍ Prepare your vehicle for evacuation (fuel tank full, emergency kit in car).

❍ Follow evacuation orders promptly; do NOT drive through flooded roads.

7. Safety During a Flood

❍ Avoid walking or driving through moving floodwaters; six inches of water can knock you down, and one foot can sweep a vehicle away.

- ❍ If trapped in moving water, float on your back and move with the current to safety.
- ❍ Use life jackets or flotation devices if available.
- ❍ Avoid contact with floodwater when possible; it may be contaminated.
- ❍ If sheltering in place, move to the highest level or safest room.
- ❍ Keep emergency supplies within reach.
- ❍ Maintain communication with family, neighbors, and emergency responders.
- ❍ Conserve battery power on devices and use emergency radios to stay informed.

8. After the Flood: Recovery and Restoration

- ❍ Do NOT enter your home until authorities declare it safe.
- ❍ Inspect for structural damage before entering.
- ❍ Wear protective clothing: boots, gloves, masks.
- ❍ Check for gas leaks, electrical hazards, and sewage contamination.
- ❍ Document all damages with photos and videos for insurance claims.
- ❍ Begin water removal and drying using pumps, dehumidifiers, and fans.
- ❍ Remove wet materials promptly to prevent mold growth.
- ❍ Clean and disinfect all surfaces to reduce health risks.
- ❍ Use appropriate mold removal methods or hire professionals if mold is extensive.
- ❍ Contact your insurance company to file claims immediately.
- ❍ Apply for disaster assistance from government programs if eligible.
- ❍ Seek support from community relief organizations and mental health services.
- ❍ Rebuild and repair with flood-resistant materials and techniques.
- ❍ Review and update your flood preparedness plan based on lessons learned.

9. Community Engagement and Long-Term Preparedness

- ❍ Participate in local flood preparedness training or CERT programs.
- ❍ Support community initiatives for improved drainage and flood defenses.

- ❍ Stay active in local emergency planning and neighborhood watch groups.
- ❍ Encourage local authorities to maintain and update floodplain maps and early-warning systems.
- ❍ Advocate for sustainable land use and infrastructure to reduce flood risks.
- ❍ Share your knowledge and resources with neighbors and vulnerable populations.
- ❍ Help establish or contribute to community emergency shelters and resources.

10. Mental and Emotional Preparedness

- ❍ Prepare mentally for the possibility of evacuation or loss.
- ❍ Discuss fears and plans openly with family members.
- ❍ Practice stress-reducing techniques such as deep breathing and mindfulness.
- ❍ Establish support networks to assist with anxiety or trauma.
- ❍ Know where to find professional counseling services after a disaster.

A COMPREHENSIVE GUIDE TO EMERGENCY CONTACT LISTS

Emergencies can strike without warning, disrupting everyday life and making communication difficult at best. Whether it's a flood, hurricane, wildfire, power outage, or personal crisis, having a well-prepared Emergency Contact List is a crucial step in ensuring safety, coordination, and peace of mind. This list helps you reach essential people quickly and keep everyone informed and connected during critical moments.

WHY AN EMERGENCY CONTACT LIST MATTERS

In an emergency, clear communication can make a critical difference. Having an emergency contact list ensures that vital information is quickly available, helping you act decisively when every second counts. It eliminates the need to search for phone numbers or email addresses during a crisis, and it provides alternative ways to connect when the usual communication channels are disrupted.

Beyond personal use, an emergency contact list helps coordinate a broader response. It becomes a shared tool that keeps your family, friends, neighbors, and colleagues aligned. When everyone knows whom to contact, where to go, and how to share updates, the group can work together more safely and efficiently.

This kind of preparation is especially important for households that include vulnerable populations such as children, elderly family members, or people with disabilities. A well-organized list ensures that caregivers, medical professionals, and emergency responders can be notified promptly to provide timely assistance.

Having this list ready also helps reduce stress and panic. In high-pressure situations, emotions can overwhelm decision-making. A contact list offers structure, acting as a guide that reminds you of the next steps and providing a sense of control amid uncertainty.

WHAT TO INCLUDE IN YOUR EMERGENCY CONTACT LIST

An effective emergency contact list should include a wide range of critical contacts to cover different scenarios. This may include family members, close friends, neighbors, work or school contacts, healthcare providers, local emergency services, utility companies, and any other relevant organizations. Be sure to include both primary and alternative methods of contact, such as phone numbers, email addresses, and physical addresses when necessary.

1. Immediate Family and Household Members

Include all members of your household or family, along with phone numbers, emails, and alternate contacts, if applicable.

- Full name
- Relationship (e.g., spouse, child, roommate)
- Primary phone number (mobile and/or landline)
- Secondary phone number or email
- Physical address (important if coordinating meeting points)
- Special needs or medical conditions (optional)

2. Extended Family and Close Friends

Include trusted relatives or friends who can provide support, care, or shelter if needed.

- Name
- Relationship
- Phone numbers and email
- Address (if they might serve as an evacuation point)

3. Emergency Services

These are essential numbers for immediate help during emergencies.

- 911 (or local emergency number)
- Police department (non-emergency number)
- Fire department
- Ambulance and EMS
- Poison control center
- Local emergency management office
- Animal control (if you have pets)

4. Medical Contacts

Having ready access to healthcare contacts is critical during health emergencies.

- Primary care physician(s)
- Pediatrician or specialist doctors
- Dentist

- Local hospital or urgent care center
- Pharmacy
- Mental health counselor or therapist

5. Work and School Contacts

To coordinate emergency notifications or arrange pickups.

- Employer contact (HR or direct supervisor)
- Child's school (main office, nurse's office)
- Daycare or babysitter
- Neighbor or trusted friend designated as emergency contact for children

6. Utility Companies

In cases of power outages, gas leaks, or water problems, knowing utility contacts helps resolve issues quickly.

- Electric company
- Gas company
- Water department
- Internet/cable provider

7. Insurance Companies

To report damage or file claims after disasters.

- Homeowner's insurance agent or company
- Auto insurance
- Flood insurance (if separate)
- Life insurance agent

8. Local Community and Volunteer Organizations

- Local Red Cross chapter
- Community Emergency Response Team (CERT)
- Shelters and relief organizations

9. Digital Emergency Contact List

- Store your contacts in your phone's contacts app, but create a dedicated emergency group for priority contacts. Many smartphones allow you to add emergency information accessible from the lock screen without unlocking the phone.

- Additionally, apps like Evernote, Google Keep, or dedicated emergency apps allow you to store detailed lists that can be synced across devices.

STEPS TO CREATING AN EMERGENCY CONTACT LIST

Creating a comprehensive emergency contact list is a simple but powerful step toward improving your readiness for any crisis. Follow this step-by-step guide to build a list that is accurate, accessible, and truly useful when it matters most.

DECIDE ON A FORMAT

Select the format that best suits your household and accessibility needs:

- **Paper List:** Post it in visible, high-traffic areas like the fridge, inside a cabinet door, or in an emergency binder. Keep copies in go-bags or with your emergency kit.
- **Digital List:** Save it on smartphones, tablets, or computers. Use secure cloud-based platforms for easy access from anywhere.
- **Combination Approach:** Use both paper and digital formats to ensure redundancy in case one becomes unavailable during an emergency (e.g., power outage or device failure).

You may also want to use shared apps or family planner tools that allow multiple users to view or update the list.

INCLUDE ADDITIONAL INFORMATION

To make the list even more helpful, add important contextual details:

- Priority instructions (e.g., “Contact Grandma if Mom doesn’t answer”)
- Communication preferences (e.g., “Use text during power outages”)
- Meeting points for evacuation or reunification

- Medical information like allergies, critical conditions, medications, or insurance numbers
- Pet information and vet contact details, if applicable

You may also want to include a brief "emergency protocol" summary at the top of the list with basic steps (e.g., "Check in with all family members, call 911 if needed, head to designated meeting point").

DISTRIBUTE COPIES

Keep at least three copies of your list: one in your home (fridge or emergency binder), one in your wallet/purse, and one saved digitally (phone, cloud).

Make sure your emergency contact list is accessible to everyone who may need it:

- Give printed copies to family members, babysitters, nannies, or caregivers.
- Share digital versions via email, a shared drive, or apps with roommates or household members.
- Offer a copy to trusted neighbors or friends who may assist during an emergency.

Talk through the list with children and elderly family members so they understand what it is and how to use it. During family emergency drills, practice accessing and using the contact list. This builds familiarity so it becomes second nature during real emergencies.

REGULARLY UPDATE

Review and update the list at least every six months or after major life changes (e.g., new phone numbers, new school, new doctor). Set a recurring calendar reminder to check and confirm all information. Outdated or incorrect contact information can slow down response times or lead to confusion during emergencies.

By following these steps, your emergency contact list will serve as a reliable tool that supports quick action, clear communication, and greater peace of mind when it's needed most.

EMERGENCY CONTACT LIST FOR CHILDREN

Children need a simplified, accessible version of the emergency contact list that they can understand and use independently when necessary. Keep the tone friendly and the layout clear, using large text and visuals when possible.

Include the following:

- Names and phone numbers of parents or guardians
- A trusted neighbor or nearby relative
- School contact information (main office, principal, teacher)
- Basic emergency numbers (911, poison control) with simple instructions on when to use them
- Home address and parents' full names

Tips:

- Teach children how to use the list through role-playing or brief practice sessions.
- Keep a copy in their backpack, homework folder, or near the home phone.
- If using a digital device, make sure the contact list is saved and easily accessible without a password lock.

EMERGENCY CONTACT LIST FOR PEOPLE WITH DISABILITIES OR SPECIAL NEEDS

Emergency planning must address the unique needs of people with disabilities or medical conditions to ensure they receive timely and appropriate support.

Essential components to include:

- Primary caregivers and backup contacts
- Medical providers (doctors, specialists, pharmacies)
- Details of prescribed medications, dosages, and refill information
- Notes on mobility aids, oxygen tanks, or medical equipment
- Communication preferences (e.g., sign language, assistive devices, interpreter needs)

- Emergency transport services if required (e.g., accessible transportation providers)

Tips:

- Include a copy of this customized list in a go-bag, emergency kit, or medical binder.
- Share it with caregivers, family members, and any local support organizations.
- Ensure that all emergency responders are aware of these considerations by adding a medical ID card or sticker to visible areas (e.g., refrigerator, mobility device, or entrance).

By tailoring your emergency contact list to meet the diverse needs of each individual in your household, you enhance safety, communication, and peace of mind. Preparedness is not one-size-fits-all, and your emergency plan should reflect that.

GLOSSARY

100-Year Flood: A flood event with a 1 percent chance of occurring in any given year.

Access Hatch: Waterproof entry point to crawl spaces or utility areas.

Access Road: Road designed for emergency or evacuation use during floods.

Actuarial Rate: Insurance premium based on calculated risk of flooding.

Adaptation Strategy: Long-term approach to reduce vulnerability to flooding.

After-Action Report: Review of emergency response to identify successes and areas for improvement.

Air Brick Cover: Device used to block air bricks to prevent floodwater ingress.

Alert System: Network that provides warnings about impending natural disasters.

All-Hazards Approach: Emergency planning that prepares for multiple types of disasters.

Alternate Power Source: Backup energy like solar panels or generators for use during outages.

Alternative Evacuation Route: Backup path used when main roads are flooded.

Anchor Bolts: Fasteners used to secure structures to their foundations against flood forces.

Annual Exceedance Probability (AEP): Likelihood of a flood event occurring in any given year.

Aperture Sealant: Material used to seal gaps in walls or windows.

Appraisal: Evaluation of property value; can be influenced by flood history.

Aquifer: Underground layer of water-bearing rock; may be affected by flooding.

Arroyo: Dry creek that can flood rapidly during heavy rain.

Asset Inventory: List of valuables for insurance and emergency purposes.

Asset Protection Plan: Strategy to minimize damage to valuable items.

Automatic Flood Barrier: Self-activating system that rises when flooding occurs.

Backflow Valve: Device to prevent water from flowing back into a structure through plumbing.

Backup Generator: Secondary power source in case of outages.

Barometric Pressure: Drop in pressure often signals storms or hurricanes.

Base Flood Elevation (BFE): The height floodwaters are expected to rise during a base flood.

Base Isolation: Building technique that reduces structural movement during disasters.

Basement Waterproofing: Techniques used to prevent water from entering a basement.

Batten Down: To secure objects in preparation for a storm or flood.

Battery Backup: A secondary power source for sump pumps or critical electronics during outages.

Battery Pack: Portable device used to charge electronics without wall power.

Benchmark Flood: A historical flood used as a reference point.

Benefit-Cost Ratio (BCR): Metric used to assess cost-effectiveness of flood mitigation projects.

Biodegradable Sandbag: Eco-friendly sandbag alternative.

Bleeder Drain: Drain system to relieve water pressure under a foundation.

Blue Alert: Notification system for severe weather-related law enforcement alerts.

Boil Water Advisory: Public warning that water may be contaminated after a flood.

Boundary Map: Official map defining floodplain or flood zone edges.

Breakaway Wall: Wall designed to give way under floodwaters, preventing structural damage.

Breakline: Line on a map indicating sudden changes in elevation, often affecting flood behavior.

Building Envelope: The physical barrier between the interior and exterior of a home.

Buoyancy Control: Measures to keep tanks or structures from floating in floodwaters.

Buyout Program: Government purchase of flood-prone homes for demolition or conversion to open space.

Carbon Monoxide Poisoning: A deadly risk from using gas-powered devices in enclosed spaces.

Catch Basin: In-ground container that collects runoff and directs it to drainage systems.

Channelization: Altering natural water flow through man-made channels.

Check Valve: Prevents reverse flow in pipes during flooding.

Cistern: Large tank used to store rainwater; may overflow during floods.

Cladding: Exterior covering of a structure; some are flood-resistant.

Claim: A formal request for payment from your insurance provider.

Climate Change: Long-term alteration in weather patterns affecting flood frequency.

Climate Resilience: Ability to withstand or recover from climate-related events like floods.

Coastal Flooding: Flooding due to storm surge or high tides.

Code Compliance: Meeting local building codes for flood resistance.

Community Emergency Response Team (CERT): Volunteers trained to assist in emergencies.

Community Rating System (CRS): FEMA program that rewards flood-prepared communities with lower insurance rates.

Compensatory Storage: Volume replacement for displaced floodwater due to construction.

Confined Space Hazard: Danger in small, enclosed areas that may fill with water.

Contents Coverage: Insurance coverage for personal belongings damaged in a flood.

Contingency Plan: Backup plan for emergencies or unexpected situations.

Continuity Plan: A plan to continue operations after a disaster.

Conveyance: Ability of floodwater to move through an area.

Conveyance Capacity: Amount of water a channel or pipe can carry.

Coordination Center: Hub for emergency management operations.

Coverage Limit: Maximum amount an insurance company will pay on a claim.

Crawl Space Encapsulation: Sealing of crawl spaces to protect from moisture and flooding.

Critical Depth: Depth of flow in open channel at minimum energy.

Critical Infrastructure: Facilities essential for public safety (e.g., hospitals, power plants).

Culvert: Tunnel allowing water to flow under a road; blockage can cause flooding.

Curb Inlet: Opening at street level to divert runoff into the sewer system.

Damage Assessment Team: Officials who evaluate flood damage post-event.

Dead Load: Weight of a structure without movable objects; important for stability in floods.

Debris: Flood-borne objects that pose hazards.

Debris Flow: Fast-moving mass of water and debris.

Decontamination Zone: Area designated for cleaning people and equipment post-flood.

Deductible: The amount the policyholder must pay before insurance kicks in.

Dehumidifier: Appliance that removes moisture from the air to prevent mold.

Design Flood Elevation (DFE): Level that a building must be elevated above, based on expected flood risk.

Disaster Declaration: Official recognition of a disaster, allowing access to aid.

Disaster Recovery Center (DRC): FEMA-run location where flood victims access assistance.

Disaster Relief: Aid provided after a declared disaster, often from government programs.

Displacement: Temporary or permanent relocation due to flooding.

Diversion Channel: Man-made channel redirecting floodwaters away from homes.

Diversion Dam: Structure redirecting water to reduce flood risk downstream.

Door Dam: Removable flood barrier installed across a doorway.

Drainage Basin: Area where all water drains to a common outlet.

Drainage Swale: Shallow trench designed to redirect stormwater.

Drainage System: Infrastructure that redirects water to prevent flooding.

Dry Floodproofing: Measures to keep floodwater out of buildings.

Dry Storage: Elevated storage of goods to protect them from floodwater.

Dryproofing: Making a structure watertight below the base flood elevation.

Easement: Legal right for infrastructure like levees or drains to access land.

Electrical Panel: Central distribution point for a home's electrical system; should be elevated.

Elevation Certificate: Document verifying a building's elevation for insurance purposes.

Emergency Alert System (EAS): Nationwide system for broadcasting urgent messages.

Emergency Broadcast: Official updates via radio/TV during disasters.

Emergency Evacuation Plan: Route and instructions for quickly exiting a property or area.

Emergency Kit: A set of supplies prepared in case of evacuation or sheltering.

Emergency Management Agency: Local/state group responsible for disaster coordination.

Emergency Preparedness Kit: Prepacked supplies for surviving a flood.

Emergency Radio: Battery or crank-operated radio for receiving updates during outages.

Emergency Shelter: Temporary housing during and after a flood.

Encroachment: Illegal building or development into floodplain areas.

Erosion: Wearing away of land by water, often worsened by flooding.

Erosion Control Fabric: Textile used to prevent soil loss during floods.

Evacuation Drill: Practice session for fleeing a flood threat.

Evacuation Order: Official instruction to leave a hazardous area.

Evacuation Route: Preplanned and marked paths for leaving flood-prone areas.

Excess Flood Insurance: Additional coverage beyond NFIP limits.

Expanded Polystyrene (EPS) Blocks: Lightweight fill for raising land or foundations.

Exposure: The degree to which people or property are likely to be affected by flood.

Exposure Risk: Level of danger a property faces from potential flood events.

Exposure Time: Duration of vulnerability to flood conditions.

Extended Coverage: Optional insurance add-ons beyond standard policies.

Fast-Rising Flood: Rapid onset flood, often with minimal warning.

Federal Coordinating Officer (FCO): FEMA appointee in charge of disaster response.

Federal Emergency Management Agency (FEMA): US agency for disaster response and flood mapping.

FEMA Disaster Assistance: Federal support for those affected by major floods.

FEMA Flood Map Service Center: Online portal for FEMA flood maps.

Field Moisture Sensor: Measures soil saturation to forecast potential flooding.

Fill Material: Soil or gravel used to raise land elevation in flood zones.

Fill Permit: Required permission for raising ground level in flood zones.

First Responder: Emergency personnel who assist during disasters.

First-Aid Kit: Supplies to treat minor injuries and prevent infections.

Flash Flood: Sudden and intense flood event caused by heavy rain.

Flash Point: Lowest temperature at which vapors ignite; relevant in flood-related fuel leaks.

Flashlight: Critical item in blackout situations.

Flashlight Beacon: Flashlight with strobe setting for signaling rescue teams.

Flotation Device: Safety tool to keep individuals buoyant in water.

Flood Adaptation: Adjustments made to cope with flood threats.

Flood Alert Level: Severity scale indicating potential impact of flooding.

Flood Alert System App: Mobile app providing real-time flood alerts.

Flood Alert Zone: Region under surveillance due to rising water levels.

Flood Barrier: Temporary or permanent structures to block floodwater.

Flood Basin: Depressed area designed to contain floodwater.

Flood Damage: Destruction caused directly by floodwaters.

Flood Data Logger: Device tracking water levels and flood conditions over time.

Flood Diary: Personal log used to document flood impacts for recovery or claims.

Flood Forecasting: Predicting future flood events using data models.

Flood Gate: Movable barrier used to control water flow.

Flood Hazard Area: Region officially recognized as prone to flooding.

Flood Insurance: Special insurance covering damage caused by flooding.

Flood Mitigation Device: Any tool used to reduce flood impact (e.g., vent, barrier).

Flood Mitigation Grant: Government funds for reducing flood risk.

Flood Recovery Timeline: Projected schedule for returning to normal after flooding.

Flood Resilience: Ability of a property to withstand or quickly recover from flooding.

Flood Resistor: Device used to block floodwater entry through pipes or vents.

Flood Retention Pond: Artificial pond to hold floodwater.

Flood Risk Assessment: Evaluation of the probability and impact of flooding.

Flood Risk Communication Plan: Strategy to inform the public about flood hazards.

Flood Stage: The level at which a river will overflow its banks.

Flood-Tolerant Materials: Construction materials that withstand water exposure.

Flood Vent: Opening in foundations to allow floodwater to pass through safely.

Flood Warning: Notification that flooding is imminent or occurring.

Flood Watch: Notification that flooding is possible.

Flood Way: Part of the floodplain that carries fast-moving water.

Flood Zone: FEMA-designated area with specific flood risk.

Floodplain: Flat area near a river prone to flooding.

Floodplain Encroachment: Development that reduces flood storage or flow capacity.

Floodplain Management: Regulation and planning to reduce flood impacts.

Floodplain Map: A visual representation of flood-prone areas.

Floodproofing: Strategies to reduce flood damage to buildings.

Floodproofing Certificate: Document proving a building's flood defenses.

Foam Core Door: Lightweight, water-resistant door for flood-prone buildings.

Forebay: Pre-settling area to capture sediment before stormwater enters a pond.

Foundation: Base of a home; important for structural flood resistance.

Foundation Drain: Subsurface drainage that prevents water buildup around a foundation.

Freeboard: Extra height added to flood protection design.

Frequent Flood Zone: Area that floods multiple times per year.

Gabion: Cage filled with rocks used for erosion control.

Gas Shut-Off Valve: Manual or automatic valve to prevent gas leaks during flooding.

Generator: Machine for producing power during outages.

Geographic Information System (GIS): Mapping system used to assess flood risk.

Groundwater Seepage: Water infiltrating belowground levels during or after a flood.

Hazard Insurance: Coverage for disasters; may exclude floods unless added.

Hazard Mitigation: Actions to reduce or eliminate flood damage.

Hazard Zone: Area exposed to natural dangers like floods or landslides.

Heat Map: Visual representation of flood risk or damage levels.

High-Frequency Warning System: Alert system for rapidly developing floods.

High-Water Mark: Line marking the highest point floodwaters reached.

Home Elevation Grant: Assistance for raising homes above flood levels.

Home Inventory Software: Digital tool for tracking home belongings.

Homeowner's Insurance: General insurance that typically excludes flood coverage.

House Raising: Elevating an entire home above flood level.

Humidity: Moisture in the air; contributes to mold growth post-flood.

Hurricane: Large storm system with heavy rains and strong winds.

Hydraulic Load: The amount of water force exerted on a structure.

Hydrology Study: Research analyzing water flow and flood potential.

Impact Assessment: Study of the potential effects of flooding.

Impact-Resistant Glass: Windows that can withstand debris during storms.

Impervious Surface: Surface (like pavement) that prevents water absorption.

Incident Command System (ICS): Structured approach to disaster response.

Inclement Weather Policy: Plan outlining employee or resident procedures during flooding.

Infiltration: Water entering a building through leaks or cracks.

Infiltration Basin: Depression in land where runoff is allowed to seep into the ground.

Ingress and Egress: Ability to enter or exit a building or area safely.

Insurance Adjuster: Evaluates damages and determines claim payments.

Insurance Deductible: Amount paid out of pocket before insurance kicks in.

Insurance Exclusion: Specific situations or damages not covered by a policy.

Inundation: Complete submersion of land in water.

Land Subsidence: Gradual sinking of ground, increasing flood risk.

Landslide Triggering: Floods loosening soil and causing collapses.

Large-Diameter Sump Pump: Heavy-duty pump for severe basement flooding.

Leach Field: Part of a septic system; can fail during floods.

Levee: Barrier built to prevent river overflow.

Life Vest: Wearable device to aid buoyancy in water.

Lifeline Services: Essential utilities like power, water, and communications.

Load Path Continuity: Engineering design ensuring structural stability during floods.

Local Hazard Mitigation Plan: Community strategy to reduce flood risk.

Low-Impact Development (LID): Development designed to manage stormwater naturally.

Low-Lying Area: Region more susceptible to flooding due to lower elevation.

Marshland: Wetland area often acting as a flood buffer.

Mildew: Fungal growth similar to mold; thrives in damp environments.

Mitigation: Measures taken to reduce flood damage.

Mitigation Bank: Restoration of wetlands to offset development impacts.

Mobile App Alert System: Smartphone apps for real-time emergency updates.

Moisture Barrier: Layer preventing water from entering walls or floors.

Mold: Fungal growth resulting from prolonged moisture exposure.

Mold Remediation: Professional or DIY method to remove mold.

Muck-Out: Process of removing mud and debris after floodwaters recede.

Multi-Tool: Versatile tool useful during emergencies.

Mutual Aid Agreement: Regional agreement for sharing emergency resources.

Narrow Channel Flow: High-speed water movement through constricted spaces.

National Flood Insurance Program (NFIP): Government-run flood insurance provider.

National Resilience Index: Metric showing a community's preparedness level.

National Weather Service (NWS): US agency providing flood forecasts.

Natural Disaster: Severe natural event, such as a flood or hurricane.

Negative Pressure Zone: Area where suction can draw in floodwater.

NOAA: National Oceanic and Atmospheric Administration; provides flood maps and alerts.

No-Build Zone: Area where construction is prohibited due to flood risk.

Nonperishable Food: Food that doesn't spoil quickly; crucial in emergencies.

Nonstructural Measures: Flood risk reduction methods that don't involve construction.

Occupant Load: Number of people a shelter or home can safely support.

Outfall: Exit point for water in a drainage system.

Overflow: When water exceeds the capacity of a system or container.

Overflow Alarm: Device that alerts when water levels breach safety thresholds.

Permeable Surface: Material that allows water to pass through.

Pet Carrier: Transport container for pets during evacuation.

Policy Limits: The maximum benefits your flood policy offers.

Portable Charger: Power bank for mobile devices.

Pre-Disaster Inspection: Evaluation of home conditions before flooding occurs.

Preparedness Drill: Practice scenario for responding to a disaster.

Preparedness Plan: Strategy for what to do before, during, and after a flood.

Prescriptive Code: Building rule specifying exact methods for flood protection.

Private Flood Insurance: Non-government insurance policies that cover flood damage.

Rain Gauge: Tool for measuring rainfall; used in flood forecasting.

Rapid Deployment Flood Barrier: Quick-install system for last-minute flood protection.

Rapid-Onset Flood: Flood that occurs with little to no warning, often within hours.

Real Estate Disclosure: Requirement to inform buyers of past flood damage.

Rebuild Value: The cost to reconstruct a home after destruction.

Reconstruction: Rebuilding a property after flood damage.

Recovery Coordination Officer (RCO): FEMA role managing long-term recovery efforts.

Red Tagging: Labeling a building unsafe to enter post-disaster.

Redevelopment: New construction on previously flooded or developed land.

Reentry Permit: Government-issued approval to return to an evacuated area.

Regulatory Floodway: Channel designated to carry base flood without obstruction.

Reinforced Roof: Roof structure built to withstand heavy rain and winds.

Relocation Grant: Financial assistance to move permanently out of a flood zone.

Rescue Operations: Emergency actions to save people during floods.

Rescue Swimmer: Trained emergency worker who saves individuals in water.

Resettlement Assistance: Help provided to people permanently displaced.

Resilience: The capacity to recover from a flood event.

Resilience Planning: Long-term strategy to improve community flood resistance.

Retention Pond: Man-made basin that holds stormwater to prevent flooding.

Retrofit: Modifications to improve a building's flood resistance.

Reverse 911 System: Community alert system that calls residents in emergencies.

Risk Communication: Sharing information about flood threats and actions.

Risk Reduction Measure: Any action that lessens flood danger or damage.

Risk Zone A: High-risk flood area according to FEMA.

River Gauge: Device measuring water level in a river.

Riverine Flood: Flooding caused by overflowing rivers.

Roof Strapping: Method to secure roofs against uplift from high winds.

Rooftop Drain: Drainage point on roofs to prevent water accumulation.

Runoff: Water that flows over land, contributing to flooding.

Runoff Coefficient: Measure of how much rainfall becomes surface runoff.

Safe Room: Reinforced area designed to protect occupants during extreme weather.

Safety Perimeter: Zone established around hazardous areas post-flood.

Sand Boil: Eruption of water and sand due to pressure under levees.

Sandbag: Temporary flood barrier made from sacks of sand.

Sandbag Wall: Temporary structure built with sandbags to block water.

Sanitation: Preventing disease through cleanliness post-flood.

Satellite Emergency Map: Aerial imagery used to assess flooding and damage.

Scour: Erosion of soil near foundation or structure caused by fast-moving water.

Secondary Containment: Backup system to prevent hazardous spills during floods.

Sediment Load: The amount of particles carried by floodwaters.

Seepage: Slow water intrusion through walls or foundation.

Seepage Barrier: Subsurface structure that prevents water from penetrating foundations.

Sensor Network: Grid of monitoring devices tracking water levels and flood activity.

Sewer Backup: When stormwater overwhelms sewage systems.

Sheltering Needs Assessment: Evaluation of how many and what types of shelters are required.

Shelter-in-Place: Strategy to remain indoors during an emergency.

Shelter-in-Place Order: Official directive to remain indoors during a flood.

Shock Hazard: Risk of electrocution from waterlogged electrical systems.

Short-Term Rental Restrictions: Flood zone rules limiting vacation or Airbnb-style rentals.

Siding: Exterior material of a home that can be flood-resistant.

Silt: Fine sediment often deposited inside homes after flooding.

Silt Fence: Temporary barrier used to control sediment in flood-prone areas.

Simultaneous Hazards: Occurrence of flood and another disaster (e.g., fire, landslide).

Siren Alert System: Outdoor system warning of incoming floods.

Site Drainage Plan: Blueprint showing how water will flow on a property.

Slab-On-Grade Foundation: Concrete slab directly on the ground; vulnerable in floods.

Slope Failure: Collapse of sloped ground due to water saturation.

Sluice Gate: Water control structure used in urban drainage.

Smart Leak Detector: Sensor that alerts users to water intrusion in real time.

Soakaway Pit: Underground system allowing water to gradually drain into soil.

Spillway: Structure that safely releases excess water from a dam or levee.

Standing Orders: Preauthorized flood response procedures.

Storm Drainage System: Network that channels rainwater to prevent street flooding.

Storm Surge: Rise in sea level caused by a storm or hurricane.

Stormwater Diversion: Redirecting excess rainwater to avoid flooding.

Structural Floodproofing: Permanent physical changes to prevent water entry.

Structural Measures: Physical infrastructure to control flood risk (dams, levees).

Subfloor Drainage System: Installed beneath flooring to redirect water away.

Submersible Pump: Waterproof pump used in flood cleanup.

Subsidized Insurance: Government-supported insurance to make premiums more affordable.

Sump Pump: Device that removes water accumulating in a basement.

Surface Runoff: Rainwater that flows over land rather than soaking in.

Surge Protector: Device that protects electronics from power spikes.

Sustainable Drainage System (SuDS): Modern water management system reducing urban flood risk.

Swale: Shallow channel guiding water runoff away from structures.

Sway Testing: Structural test simulating wind or water movement.

Temporary Housing Assistance: FEMA or NGO-supported short-term accommodation aid.

Temporary Relocation: Short-term move due to flooding of home or community.

Temporary Shelter: Emergency housing after displacement.

Tensile Strength: Material's resistance to breaking under pressure; important for flood barriers.

Thermal Imaging Camera: Used to detect water infiltration behind walls.

Threshold Barrier: Flood guard placed at doorways.

Through-Flow Vent: Allows water to pass through a structure without damage.

Tide Surge: Sudden rise in seawater due to storm.

Tile Drain System: Underground pipes to manage excess water near foundations.

Topographic Map: Map showing elevation, helpful in flood risk analysis.

Tornado + Flood Risk Zones: Overlapping hazard areas requiring complex mitigation.

Toxic Floodwater: Water contaminated by chemicals, sewage, or industrial waste.

Trapped Air Pockets: Air gaps in flooded buildings that can pose risk or offer refuge.

Triage Area: Medical treatment zone set up in emergency shelters.

Tropical Depression: Weak tropical storm that may still cause flooding.

Turbidity: Cloudiness of floodwater indicating contamination or sediment.

Undermining: Erosion beneath a structure causing instability.

Universal Design: Accessible home design helpful in emergencies for disabled individuals.

Unreinforced Masonry: Brickwork without steel reinforcement; more flood-prone.

Upstream Flooding: Overflow occurring at the headwaters of rivers or streams.

Urban Flooding: Flooding caused by heavy rainfall in city infrastructure.

Urban Heat Island Effect: Heat-trapping effect that can exacerbate evaporation and rainfall.

Urban Runoff: Stormwater that collects in cities, often leading to flash floods.

Utility Elevation Platform: Raised structure for placing electrical and HVAC units.

Vacuum Sewer System: Alternative plumbing system for flood-prone areas.

Vapor Barrier: Material preventing moisture from entering structures.

Ventilation: Airflow to prevent mold buildup.

Ventilation Grate Flood Cover: Protective lid for air grates during floods.

Vulnerability Assessment: Analysis of who and what is at risk during a flood.

Vulnerable Populations: Groups most at risk in disasters (e.g., elderly, infants, disabled).

V-Zone: FEMA term for coastal high-velocity flood zone.

Wading Depth Limit: Maximum safe depth for walking through water.

Wall Anchors: Reinforcements preventing collapse due to hydrostatic pressure.

Warning Coordination Meteorologist (WCM): NOAA expert who helps local areas plan.

Warning Time: Time between a flood alert and actual flooding.

Water Alarm Sensor: Device that sounds an alert upon detecting moisture.

Water Damage Exclusion: Clause in policies that limits coverage for water-related loss.

Water Damage Restoration: Process of repairing and drying out a flood-damaged home.

Water Depth Gauge: Tool used to monitor rising flood levels.

Water Entry Point: Common locations where water infiltrates a structure.

Water Line Staining: Mark left by standing water indicating flood height.

Water Removal Crew: Team specialized in post-flood extraction and drying.

Water Table Level: Height of groundwater; affects basement flooding potential.

Waterproof Container: Storage solution that keeps contents dry.

Watershed: Area of land that drains into a particular body of water.

Watershed Map: Map showing drainage basins contributing to flood zones.

Wave Action: Oscillating water movement that increases coastal flood risk.

Weather App: Tool for tracking storms and floods.

Weather Radio (NOAA): Battery-powered device that broadcasts emergency alerts.

Weatherproof Container: Storage that resists moisture and flooding.

Weatherproofing: Strengthening a building against weather extremes.

Wellhead Protection: Safeguarding private wells from contaminated floodwater.

Wet Floodproofing: Allowing floodwater into a structure but minimizing damage.

Wetproofing: Accepting water entry but designing a structure to minimize damage.

Wind Load: Force exerted on a building by wind; relevant during hurricanes.

Wind-Driven Rain: Rain blown horizontally, which can enter sealed structures.

Window Well Cover: Plastic or metal dome preventing water from filling basement wells.

Worksite Flood Plan: Company-specific protocol for responding to flooding.

Zero Net Fill Policy: Rule requiring no increase in elevation that would worsen flooding.

Zone AE: FEMA flood zone with known elevation levels.

Zone AO: FEMA flood zone with shallow flooding risks.

Zone D: Area with unstudied flood risks.

Zone X: FEMA designation for areas of minimal flood risk.

Zoned Evacuation: Evacuating based on geographic flood risk levels.

Zoning Ordinance: Law controlling land use in flood-prone regions.

Zoning Overlay: Special area with added regulations due to flood or hazard risk.

Zoning Regulations: Laws determining building permissions in flood-prone areas.

Zoning Setback: Required distance between a building and floodplain boundary.

Zoning Variance: Exception to zoning rules, sometimes granted in flood-prone areas.

Zoning Violation: Building or use that contradicts floodplain regulations.

BIBLIOGRAPHY

American Red Cross. *Home Flood Safety and Preparedness Guide.* American Red Cross, 2023.

Automobile Association of America (AAA). *Flood Damage: Protecting Your Vehicle.* Automobile Association of America, 2022.

Canadian Hearing Society and DLR Consulting. *Barrier-Free Emergency Communication Access and Alerting System Research Report.* Canadian Hearing Society, March 2018.

Centers for Disease Control and Prevention (CDC). *Mold After a Disaster.* Centers for Disease Control and Prevention, 2020.

Climate.gov. "2017 US Billion-Dollar Weather and Climate Disasters: A Historic Year in Context." January 8, 2018. https://www.climate.gov/disasters-2017.

Department of Homeland Security. *Tips for Effectively Communicating with the Whole Community in Emergency Preparedness and Response.* US Department of Homeland Security, 2024.

Department of Homeland Security and Federal Emergency Management Agency (FEMA). *Crisis & Emergency Risk Communication (CERC) Manual.* FEMA, 2022.

Department of Homeland Security and Federal Emergency Management Agency (FEMA). *National Emergency Communications Plan.* US Department of Homeland Security, July 2008.

Federal Emergency Management Agency (FEMA). *Are You Ready? An In-Depth Guide to Citizen Preparedness (IS-22).* FEMA, 2004.

Federal Emergency Management Agency (FEMA). *Community Rating System (CRS)*. FEMA, accessed 2025. https://www.fema.gov/floodplain-management/community-rating-system.

Federal Emergency Management Agency (FEMA), Office of Disability Integration and Coordination (ODIC). *Disability Integration*. FEMA, last updated January 24, 2024.

Federal Emergency Management Agency (FEMA). *Flood Map Service Center*. FEMA, accessed 2025. https://msc.fema.gov/portal/home.

Federal Emergency Management Agency (FEMA). "Floods." Accessed October 6, 2025. https://ready.gov/floods.

Federal Emergency Management Agency (FEMA). *Flood Safety Tips and Resources*. US Department of Homeland Security, 2023.

Federal Emergency Management Agency (FEMA). *Guidance on Planning for Integration of Functional Needs Support Services in General Population Shelters*. FEMA, accessed November 2010.

Federal Emergency Management Agency (FEMA). *Mitigation Ideas: A Resource for Reducing Risk to Natural Hazards*. FEMA, January 2013.

Federal Emergency Management Agency (FEMA) and Maryland Department of Disabilities. *Planning for People with Disabilities and Others with Access and Functional Needs Toolkit*. FEMA and Maryland Department of Disabilities, June 2017 (updated).

Federal Emergency Management Agency (FEMA). *Homeowner's Guide to Retrofitting: Six Ways to Protect Your Home from Flooding*. Publication FEMA P-312. FEMA, July 2020.

Federal Emergency Management Agency (FEMA). *National Disaster Recovery Framework, Second Edition*. FEMA, 2020.

Federal Emergency Management Agency (FEMA). *National Flood Insurance Program (NFIP)*. FEMA, accessed 2025. https://www.fema.gov/flood-insurance.

Floodsmart.gov. "Historical NFIP Claims Information and Trends." FEMA, last accessed October 14, 2025. https://www.floodsmart.gov/historical-nfip-claims-information-and-trends?map=countries/us/custom/us-all-territories®ion=us&miny=all&maxy=all&county=>ype=country.

Florida Building Commission. *Florida Building Code & Miami-Dade High-Velocity Hurricane Zone (HVHZ) Standards*. Florida Building Commission, 2021.

Gold, Adam, and Ivy Steinburg-McElroy. "High-Resolution Estimates of the US Population in Fluvial or Coastal Flood Hazard Areas." *Scientific Data* 12, no. 1377 (2025). https://www.nature.com/articles/s41597-025-05717-y.

Institute of Inspection, Cleaning and Restoration Certification (IICRC). *Standards for Water Damage Restoration*. IICRC, 2019.

Insurance Information Institute. *Flood Insurance: What You Need to Know*. Insurance Information Institute, 2021.

National Flood Insurance Program (NFIP). *Understanding Your Flood Insurance Policy*. FEMA, 2022.

National Institute of Building Sciences. "National Institute of Building Sciences Issues Interim Report on the Value of Mitigation." January 8, 2019. https://nibs.org/national-institute-of-building-sciences-issues-interim-report-on-the-value-of-mitigation.

National Institute of Standards and Technology (NIST). *Guidelines on Flood Damage to Electrical Systems in Buildings*. NIST, 2018.

National Oceanic and Atmospheric Administration (NOAA). *Flood Risk Assessment Tools and Coastal Wetlands Research*. NOAA, accessed 2025. https://coast.noaa.gov/stormwater-floods/assess.

National Oceanic and Atmospheric Administration (NOAA). *Hurricane Preparedness and Safety*. NOAA, 2022.

Nature Conservancy. "Coastal Wetlands Provide Significant Flood Damage Reduction." *Coastal Resilience*. Accessed September 17, 2025. https://coastalresilience.org/coastal-wetlands-provide-significant-flood-damage-reduction.

National Weather Service. "Hurricane Katrina—A Look Back 20 Years Later." Accessed October 6, 2025. https://www.weather.gov/lix/katrina_anniversary.

Ready.gov. "Evacuation." Last updated January 30, 2025. https://www.ready.gov/evacuation.

Ready.gov. *Preparing Makes Sense for People with Disabilities*. US Department of Homeland Security and FEMA, March 2020.

University of New Hampshire Psychological & Counseling Services. “What Is Grounding?” UNH Psychological & Counseling Services, 2019.

US Army Corps of Engineers (USACE). *Levee Safety Program*. USACE, 2024.

US Environmental Protection Agency (EPA). *Preventing Mold Growth After Flooding*. EPA, 2018.

US Fish and Wildlife Service. *Coastal Barrier Resources System (CBRS) Maps*. US Fish and Wildlife Service, 2016.

US Geological Survey (USGS). *Flood Risk and Hydrology Data*. USGS, 2019.

ABOUT THE AUTHOR

Ryan Lee Price, a seasoned freelance writer based in California, has made a name for himself in the tech industry and the disaster preparation publications. With a wealth of experience as an editor for various disaster-preparation magazines, such as *American Survival Guide* and *Survivor's Edge*, and having penned hundreds of articles on many outdoor topics, Ryan is a trusted voice in the realm of safety and resilience.

When he's not crafting content, Ryan enjoys spending time with his wife Kara, their children Natalie and Matthew, and their beloved German Shepard, Yukon. His passion for the outdoors and commitment to preparedness make him an invaluable resource for anyone seeking to navigate the challenges of the modern world.

OTHER BOOKS FROM ULYSSES PRESS

ulyssespress.com